# Why Preach? Why Listen?

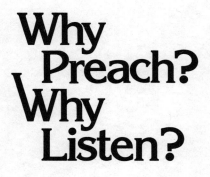

William Muehl

# Why Preach? Why Listen?

FORTRESS PRESS       PHILADELPHIA

Excerpts are reprinted by permission of The Pilgrim Press from *All the Damned Angels* by William Muehl. Copyright © 1972 United Church Press.

**Library of Congress Cataloging-in-Publication Data**

Muehl, William.
 Why preach? Why listen?

  1. Preaching. 2. Laity. I. Title.
BV4211.2.M84 1986    251    86-45216
ISBN 0-8006-1928-5

2552C86   Printed in the United States of America   1-1928

To Harry and Manette Adams
who take both the Christian Gospel
and human life seriously

# Contents

# CHAPTER 1

# Why
## a Homiletic
### Theologian?

Many years ago we had at the Yale Divinity School a student who became infatuated with Karl Barth. The works of the great Swiss theologian appealed to him in a special way. And it seemed to annoy him that not everyone shared his enthusiasm. In devotion to his idol the young man harangued seminars, gave chapel talks that were minilectures on Barth, and, when invited to preach in local churches from time to time, offered congregations forty-minute expositions of the latest volume of *Church Dogmatics.*

In spite of this single-mindedness the student eventually graduated and went forth to carry his eccentric brand of Good News to a presumably waiting world. Ten years later he returned to Yale for one of our convocations. As I chatted with him over an afternoon coffee, I noticed that he wore in his buttonhole an emblem which proclaimed him a fan of one of the nation's most popular positive-thinking media preachers, a man whose oft' repeated nostrums were about as far from the theology of Karl Barth as anything could be.

Curiosity conquered tact, and I asked my friend how he had come to so surprising a commitment in a relatively short time. He had the grace to be somewhat embarrassed, but finally and somewhat truculently he said, "I lost three churches before I learned what people want from the pulpit. So now I give it to them."

That incident has remained vivid in my mind over the years, because it is such a dramatic manifestation, such a candid confession of what many preachers seem to have experienced, often in more subtle and less painful fashion. It seems to be common for theological students to suppose that the work of doing creative theology should be finished when they graduate, that they ought to leave seminary with a ready-made message to take into the church for the edification and delight of their congregations. And that prepackaged message often and understandably reflects whatever is the current focus in seminary during the student's sojourn there. It may be Barth, social action, liberation theology, some brand of neo-biblicism, or the eccentric views of an especially charismatic teacher. Any one or a combination of carefully wrapped ways of interpreting the life of faith strikes some as going with the diploma on graduation day.

Then when the nascent preacher discovers the hard way that the people in the pews are less than enthusiastic about his or her version of someone else's thought, that even the devout tend to become first bored and then mutinous when exposed repeatedly to the latest word from academe, many young ministers abandon all serious attempt to address substantive issues of faith and begin dishing out what they would once have condemned as pure pap.

This is, to say the least, an unfortunate thing for all concerned. For the struggle of the preacher to communicate what was of value in the seminary experience can and ought to be an opportunity for *doing theology* in the most creative way. That struggle is in many respects a paradigm of the struggle of lay men and women to apply what they hear in church to the grubby and always recalcitrant details of daily life. As the pastor grapples with the relevance of classroom lectures to a complex of living room and board room problems, he or she is going through a professional version of what the laity is being called upon to do in the context of its own responsibilities and challenges in home and office.

It is, I am sure, important to remember that the people to whom we preach do not in many cases have a well-defined faith or even a poorly defined faith about which they are asking eagerly how one might apply it with greater effectiveness to the business of living. They have, for the most part, some fragmentary religious commitments that are related to one another and to some degree integrated in the give-and-take of domestic affairs, commerce, education, politics, and a host of other dynamic and demanding areas of what we like to call "the real world." And for them the flow of influence between theology and practice is a two-way process. The problem of how to be an effective and successful human being, however that is defined, and a faithful Christian does as much to fashion the *sub-*

*stance* of their faith as that substance does to shape their notions of how one witnesses to the faith in practice.

It is instructive, if somewhat dismaying, to realize how many of the men and women in the pews almost did not come to church that morning. And that in all probability most of them feel that they are there under false pretenses, that everyone around them feels more confidently Christian, less restlessly rebellious than they do themselves.

Not long ago I took part in a panel discussion of the nature and function of the local church. One of the other participants, an Episcopal priest, described the church somewhat rhapsodically as "the place in which we meet one another more honestly, share with one another more intimately, and love one another more fully than anywhere else outside the home."

As he spoke people made their faces to shine upon him and nodded benignly as those do who give assent to a time-honored truism, something that no right-thinking person would think to question. But when I got the floor a moment later I asked the audience a question. "Forget," I suggested, "that you are supposed to feel about the church as Father X has just claimed you do. How many of you really think of the church as 'the place in which you meet one another more honestly, share with one another more intimately, and love one another more fully than anywhere else outside the home?'"

In an audience of about one hundred people no more than a dozen hands went up. And one man who seemed liberated by this unusual display of candor rose to declare that he met people more honestly, shared with them more intimately, and cared for others more lovingly at the office than he ever did in church. And it became quite clear as he talked that the truly significant flow of influence in his religious life was from office to church, *not* the other way around, that he filtered and evaluated what he heard from the pulpit in terms of what he did daily at his desk.

Now it is temptingly easy to dismiss this incident as merely one more manifestation of human hypocrisy, the inability of people to live up to their professed Christian standards under the pressure of events during the week. But that would be a mistake. The man was not confessing some weakness of character which kept him from being and doing what he ought to be and do, what he really wanted in his heart of faith to be and do. He was saying, rather, that his professional relationships and commitments offered more realistic and deeply moving insights into being and doing than anything he heard from the pulpit on Sunday mornings.

In Morris West's fine novel, *The Shoes of the Fisherman,* there is a moving scene in which Pope Kyril confronts his younger friend, Father Telimond, who is surely modeled upon Pierre Teilhard de Chardin, and asks him with deep concern, "But do you really believe in the doctrines of our Holy Mother Church?"

To this Father Telimond replies, as Teilhard would probably have replied, "Yes, I believe in the doctrines of our Holy Mother Church. But I also believe in the world. First, I believe in the world."

In this, I am persuaded, Father Telimond speaks for the inarticulate masses in the Christian churches of the West. They believe in the doctrines of their churches. But they also believe in the world. First, they believe in the world. Not in the sense of being sinfully addicted to the world's cynical materialism or its own deceptive self-evaluation, but in the confidence that God is at work in that world, not simply lurking on its fringes reminding believers that they should not become too deeply engaged. In terms of the words that I shall be using in this book, they are convinced, however poorly they might say it, that God is present in the flux of their daily lives not simply as Judge and Redeemer but as Creator also. And they feel that the processes and relationships in which they spend most of their waking hours have an eternal dimension to them, a dimension in which God is as truly visible as in the weekly hour of prayer before the altar.

To put it another way, most lay men and women live in a constant and healthy tension between what they have been taught to regard as the secular and sacred realms. But there is much evidence to suggest that they understand, often better than their spiritual mentors, that God's great reconciling act on Calvary validated that tension for all time to come as the medium in which the divine will can be known and obeyed.

There is delightful irony in the fact that while preachers labor diligently week after week to make people see that they have been "accepted" by God, lay men and women tend to believe in that acceptance at a far deeper level than preachers realize. That is, they perceive that what God accepts is not the mean, nasty, and brutish aspects of our individual personalities, but the eternal significance of human life in history.

The real problem of the young man who wanted to impose Karl

Barth upon his congregations was an inability to see Barth as the starting point for the real task at hand, the inauguration of a serious conversation day after day with the deeply felt convictions flowing toward the pulpit from the pews. When his people proved unable or unwilling to swallow his prepared academic doctrine he concluded that they had no serious spiritual interests at all and began dishing out bland prudential counsels which were undoubtedly less relevant to their lives than the obscure passages of *Church Dogmatics*. He perceived as lay hostility what may have been the basis for an effective homiletic theologizing, that is, the laity's confidence in the validity of its experience as a mode of divine revelation.

The temptation to discount feedback from the congregation in such a way is understandable. And it must be admitted that the mode of its expression often encourages such an interpretation. Men and women unschooled in the protocol of theological debate are more than a little likely to adopt an adversarial style in expressing their differences with the preacher. While ministers may no longer enjoy great prestige and authority in American society generally, their status among churchgoers is likely to discourage irenic discourse. As one layman said of his pastor, "He's paid to know about such matters, and I feel a little brash arguing with him."

But while the fear of seeming "brash" may minimize the willingness to open debate over matters of fundamental belief, it does not prevent those internal dialogues in which the intimidated inevitably engage and rout their invisible opponents. And it seems unfortunately the case that these psychological victories get translated into adversarial terms in dealings between pulpit and pew. Lacking the self-confidence or the opportunity to challenge the preacher at the level of thoughtful discourse, lay men and women too often incline to lower the debate to the level of sniping at the pastor's real or alleged deficiencies in calling, counseling, working with "the youth," and other nonhomiletic responsibilities.

Consequently, the minister does not have to be paranoid in order to find substantive controversy somewhat threatening. And all too often the result is that he or she makes little effort to discover the real theological commitments that may be the true source of confrontational moods in the congregation. As unpleasant as it is, ad hominem antagonism seems easier to bear than the realization that congregations are not sold on the kind of theologizing for which their preachers got top grades in seminary.

Some years ago I was invited to speak at a corporate communion breakfast and then to stay over to preach at the eleven o'clock service of Morning Prayer. Between those two assignments there was time to kill, so the rector invited me to sit in on a class that he conducted each week on "Ethics in Business." The class consisted of about a dozen men who held positions of significance in New York City. I was able to recognize the names and faces of several from my reading of *Time* and *Newsweek*.

The discussion was remarkably dull. One after another each of those present that morning brought up an alleged ethical dilemma to which he had been exposed during the preceding week. Typical of the problems was the question of what employers should do when they suspect that their male and female employees are up to no good in the stockroom. (Put in brighter lights!)

I sat through this charade, preached my sermon, and went home. But in the middle of the following week I received the customary letter of thanks from the man who had chaired the breakfast committee and who had also been a member of the rector's class in ethics. He said the nice things appropriate to such an epistle. But then he added in a postscript in his own hand, "I'd hate to have you think that the men in this church are as stupid as we must have sounded in the rector's class," he said. "But the truth is that if we ever told that nice little man the *real* ethical dilemmas we face every day at the office, it would break his heart."

I am quite sure that the layman's diagnosis of the rector's cardiac condition was wrong, that the "nice little man" would not have been traumatized by the truth. But, and this is my point, he was not told the truth and apparently did little or nothing to discover it for himself. He and his congregation played a sort of dignified game. A priceless opportunity for real theologizing was lost, and a group of influential lay men was encouraged to feel a gentle contempt for Christian insight and priesthood.

You see, what many pastors consider "doing theology" in the ecclesiastical trenches is just one form of what Krister Stendahl called "playing Bibleland." That is, they try to get lay men and women to lift themselves by their spiritual bootstraps out of the world of their daily lives and think themselves into the ethos of Isaiah or Jeremiah, Jesus or Paul. It is a kind of neo-clericalism which sees *life* as a means of understanding *theology*, rather than the other way around.

This almost inevitably leads to a selective and shallow interpretation of human experience, one in which emphases are put upon those aspects of life which can be fitted neatly into some preset hermeneutical scheme. The given or constant is training that only the clergy possess. And the events of the laity's daily life provide illustrations or analogies by which the truths of Christianity can be demonstrated.

In a panel discussion of professional education the dean of a leading law school said, "One of our hardest jobs is to get students to think of their clients as human beings who want help in solving particular problems, not as mere opportunities for the display of their newly acquired learning." To which the representatives of medicine, dentistry, and religion said heartfelt amens. Years of study in which young men and women see individuals as case histories can generate the feeling that people exist only in consulting rooms or churches.

While this difficulty afflicts most professions to some degree, it is especially vexatious in law and theology. And it will be helpful to our present discussion to note this fact and the reason for it.

The Anglo-American common law did not originate in the deliberations of some convention gathered to write a legal code. It is the result of myriad day-to-day decisions rendered by courts in the past to settle specific conflicts between individuals. The accumulation of those decisions constitutes a body of precedent by which conduct can be guided and differences resolved.

What this means in practice is that cases argued by lawyers in the courts do not simply *clarify* existing law. They frequently result in amendments to such law and even create new law. Thus, the legal practitioner understands himself or herself as more than a mere reporter of existing rights and responsibilities and understands that he or she is in many cases breaking new ground in the area of human relationships.

Like the common law, the biblical faith was not drawn up by a convention of scholars or formulated by one person bent upon presenting the world with a complete religious system. It evolved in the course of Israel's long history, as diverse human beings perceived and responded to what they believed was the will of God active in their lives. From time to time inferences drawn from that complex body of experience and revelation were summarized in commandments and standards to guide human behavior, just as the principles of jurisprudence developed to do the same for the law.

Something of the same process describes the growth of Christian theology. The earliest representatives of the faith carried the news about Jesus Christ crucified and risen into the life of their time. As they proclaimed this gospel and sought to show its implications for particular human beings and situations, what we now perceive as Christian doctrine began to take shape. From time to time that body of experience has been summarized and rendered in creedal forms. But it began as the reaching out of the early community of faith to make the truth revealed in Christ available to men and women of varied backgrounds and needs.

Thus, the ministry of the church in every age, like the lawyer in the Anglo-American tradition, is charged to do more than merely report what has been reported and codified in the past. As clergymen and women relate in service to human beings around them, they will be engaged in a constant process of learning and sharing what they learn with those under their care. And as they do this responsibly they will be amending, if only slightly, the ways in which theology expresses the experience of God.

This process is characteristic of all aspects of ministry in every age. In counseling, teaching, and church administration the learning process goes on, as does the sharing. But it is most dramatically expressed in the preaching. As the preacher asks each week how the timeless truths revealed in Scripture can best be expounded and then related to the immediate human present, he or she will inevitably adapt familiar formulations and suggest new ways of viewing old doctrine.

It would be a mistake, I am convinced, to regard this process as merely a problem in communication in the narrow sense of that word. The preacher is called upon to do more than merely find useful words and images with which to say the same old things. The challenge is, rather, substantive. The person preparing to go into the pulpit is required to ask probing questions of himself or herself about the real meaning of those familiar formulations in a world that differs so markedly from the one in which so much doctrine took shape.

This is not a comfortable position in which to find one's self. There is something reassuring about being able to pass on unchanged the fully accepted generalizations handed down from earlier generations. And there is a lot that is intimidating about accepting responsibility for theological innovation. The words "God help me, if I preach not the gospel" are inscribed upon many pulpits and even more clerical hearts. One needs more than a dash of boldness to suppose that he or she is called to adapt the familiar generalizations rather than recapitulate them.

The extent to which preachers tend to avoid this responsibility is not determined entirely by their academic infatuation with the language and terms with which their seminary educations have taught them to think and speak about religion. It is also a reflection of the professional vice of trying to romanticize the elements of call, call first to faith and then to ministry.

Most people come to their faith commitment in ways that do not seem very impressive or spiritually edifying in retrospect. It may be that one's parents made Sunday school a weekly obligation. Perhaps the Sunday evening youth program at one of the neighborhood churches was the only dependable social occasion of an otherwise dull weekend. People have even been known to find their way to solid commitment on the basis of a gregarious desire to make a place in a new community. And the number of young men and women who first entered the house of worship on the arm of an attractive member of the opposite gender is impressively large. The roads to Christian faith are as varied as the people who profess it.

These ways seem, however, to have at least one thing in common. They are not nearly as dramatic and intellectually impressive as people feel a genuine religious experience ought to be. Understandably, most of us would like our introduction, as it were, to God to take place under auspices as significant as the relationship into which we enter. And we are not above some discreet revision of the data when the time comes to explain our faith to another. This temptation is not discouraged by the fact that so many classic stories of conversion involve the vivid elements that one would like to find in one's own.

It is not uncommon for Christians to mythologize religious phenomena. And the practice is well entrenched in the vocabulary of witnessing: some great theological book opened the eyes of faith; a dramatic encounter with the Christ present in the life of another; a hilltop communion service at summer church camp. Of this nature are the *less* contrived interpretations of the call to commitment.

One would be presumptuous, indeed, to deny that these are ever an accurate depiction of what occurred at some critical juncture in an individual's life. But it is safe to say that such experiences are not the norm, that they are more psychologically satisfying than common, and that the way to the foot of the Cross, as we often hear it called, is frequently undertaken without any conscious determination from the beginning to follow it.

When one leaves the realm of lay witness, however, and moves into the area of clerical vocations, the summons to ministry of some formal kind, then the process of mythologizing is inevitably intensified and expanded. Those who dignify their own encounters with God by discreet distortions are bound to want their clergy to have had even more dramatic awakenings. Or awakenings which, if not more dramatic, are more neatly definable. And the temptation to respond to this desire is hard to resist. Preachers find it even more embarrassing than their congregations do to acknowledge the prosy character of their special call. They seldom lie about it, but they use some of the skills acquired in their critical study of the Bible to enhance its dignity.

The net result of this revisionism on both sides of the transept is to inhibit any honest consideration of the ways in which God works in real life, as opposed to religion. Preachers tend to interpret biblical mythology in the light of their personal mythology in addressing the mythology of the laity. And the consequence is distortion compounded. The satisfyingly dramatic aspects of the biblical witness are lifted up as the normal mode of God's activity in history. And the *reality*, the prosy encounters in which the holy is perceived by most men and women, gets badly neglected.

It is not, you see, that the poetry of such discourse actually denies the prose, but that it generates an atmosphere in which the latter loses whatever qualities of drama it may have possessed and takes on a shabby dullness. Just as *real* marriage appears drab in contrast with the romantic versions with which fiction bombards us daily, so genuine religious experience suffers when it is expected to meet the vivid expectations generated by religious myths.

Let me offer a word of personal testimony here. I intended through most of my educational years to be a lawyer and did graduate from the Michigan Law School. In the course of my legal studies, however, I took part in several moot court trial arguments, the proceedings in which potential attorneys learn how to conduct themselves in the litigation of a lawsuit.

I won the cases for the most part, but the aftereffect upon my system was exceedingly painful and led to my developing what was diagnosed as a duodenal ulcer. After treating me during several of my gastric attacks, a health service doctor made an alarming prediction.

"Muehl," he said severely, "if you really undertake a career in the law, you will probably be rich by the age of forty. The only trouble is that you will be *dead* by the age of thirty."

Persuaded of the accuracy of that diagnosis of my future, I abandoned plans to become a lawyer and accepted a post at the Yale Divinity School. From the first I greatly enjoyed my teaching. But I was haunted by the uneasy feeling that I had not experienced a real call, the kind of call that I assumed had led my colleagues into their life's work. I had taken up seminary teaching because I did not have the constitution to be what I wanted to be, a trial lawyer.

One day I confessed my uneasiness to Richard Niebuhr, the distinguished but very approachable ethicist on the faculty. He heard me out, sucked for a moment on his pipe, and then laughed softly. "What does it take to make up a 'call' for you, Muehl? What you had planned to do with your life was quite literally eating you up inside, driving you, consciously or unconsciously, to consider alternatives. I can't imagine a better call outside the Bible."

Our desire to spiritualize the experience of God makes it difficult to be as realistic as Niebuhr was that day. Even when we do not engage in deliberate mythologizing we are likely to offer our testimony within the traditional language structures of theology, which can amount to the same thing in the end. When we do this often enough we may reach a state in which we become unable to remember the "way it was" and accept the standard version as the full facts.

This kind of subtle dishonesty is a form of clericalism far more detrimental to effective preaching than any of the more sacerdotal versions of the vice. Having successfully disguised the details of our religious odysseys, we preachers can become increasingly incapable of perceiving the ways in which the laity recapitulates to some degree our own journeys.

I remember talking one time with a minister friend about a young physician who was an active member of his congregation. The pastor was troubled because the doctor was quite open about his agnosticism. He had little use for firm notions about the existence of God and the authority of Scripture. When asked to explain his participation in religious services and miscellaneous programs of the church he simply said, "I want my children to grow up surrounded by the sort of people they will meet in church."

The pastor's response to this was that it represented the worst kind of culture Christianity. And he felt a responsibility to set the physician straight. The desire to have one's children grow up surrounded by Christians was simply not a sufficient reason for church membership.

To my retrospective embarrassment I was young enough then to agree with the official view and urged the clergyman to confront the sinner boldly. But with the passage of the years I have come to see that here was a wealth of opportunity for genuine theological discussion in the doctor's position. Not the kind that would earn high marks for a term paper on the Westminster Confession, but the kind that might reach, deepen, and enrich a particular human life. The fact that the young man coveted Christian company for his offspring, the flesh of his flesh, revealed something about his view of things that may well have denied his alleged agnosticism. And that possibility needed thoughtful theological discussion.

The reason that this possibility escaped both my clerical friend and me is that we were in the business of trying to fit religious experience into the experience and vocabularies that gave a certain dignity to our own confessions. Having deliberately lost touch with the trivia of which our own journeys to the Cross were composed, we could not recognize them when they cropped up in the stories of others.

C. S. Lewis has written that a critical point in his journey of faith was what he called "the conversion of the imagination," that is, the moment at which he began to look at what the world alleges are prosaic and mundane data and to see in them revelations of something vastly more richly significant than appears at first glance. This is a faculty that all Christians should cultivate, but it is especially important for those called to minister to the needs of others. For when the preacher begins to deal honestly *and* imaginatively with the data of his or her own growth in faith, the possibility of effective homiletic theologizing is immeasurably increased.

Now it would be wrong to infer from what I have been saying that one does theology in preaching by simply *sharing* his or her own experiences of God. The great variety of divine self-disclosures in history make that a narrowing and dubious process. Every responsible preacher must live in a tension between his or her personal encounters with the divine and those traditional theological formulations which have been distilled and codified from the encounters of others with that majestic and mysterious power. My exhortation is not that these doctrinal formulas be discarded or ignored but that they be heard as one set of voices in a harmony of which the subjective is also an important part.

My younger brother was at one time a member of his high school glee club. He sang second tenor and sometimes drove the rest of the family to distraction by going around whistling or humming what seemed to be tuneless sequences of notes, notes that apparently went nowhere and did not form any kind of audible melody. What he was doing was rehearsing the second tenor part of some number that the glee club was scheduled to render. The notes made harmonic sense to him because he was hearing in his mind's ear the other parts that combined to make up the finished composition. For those who lacked this harmonic background, however, his whistling was simply a distracting noise.

It is the same with the witness of one's own experience of God. It is vitally important. But it needs to be set amid the myriad other testimonies, both contemporary and traditional, which are summed up in the historic confessions and creeds of the church through the ages. To do theology in the context and with the content of the common life is not to cast carelessly aside the ways in which other and greater men and women have done the same thing. It is, rather, to take seriously the contributions of one's own experiences and relationships to the *substance* and not simply the *form* of an effective proclamation. And as one preacher after another has discovered, often with great surprise, the more seriously one takes one's prosaic encounters with the divine, the more relevant and persuasive become the doctrinal statements with which our forebears have attempted to do the same thing. No scholarly defense of traditional Christian formulations is as effective as the testimony of life itself, when life is taken seriously.

One may want to argue with ancestral confessions, amend or even discard them finally in the light of new vision. The one thing that cannot be done safely is to *ignore* them. They are woven into the fabric of those experiences which bring each of us to an understanding of human existence. To reject them out of hand is as dangerous as it is to preach them in isolation from the data of personal history.

A colleague of mine once told of an old farmer who, following a visit to the city, complained about urban dietary habits. "Take what city folks eat fer breakfast," he suggested. "Orange juice, cold cereal, toast, and instant coffee. That kind of stuff don't stay by ye. It digests an' lets ye down when ye need it most. But the old-fashioned farm breakfast, oatmeal, fried eggs, hash browns, a slab of ham, corn bread, and a stack of flapjacks, that kind of food don't digest on ye. All day long while yer workin' out in the fields ye can feel it settin' down there a-nourishin' ye and a-nourishin' ye."

Preachers too often incline to replicate the old farmer's mistake and suppose that theology does its proper work only so long as you can feel it sitting in your mind in an identifiable, indigestible mass. But it is, on the contrary, the proper task of the preacher as theologian to facilitate the digestion of Christian experience so that it becomes part of the flesh and blood of a living faith.

# CHAPTER 2

# Confessing
## the Complexity
## of Faith

Shortly after I began teaching homiletics, I was guest speaker at a service club luncheon. My presence gave several members of the organization a chance to express their feelings about the current state of Christian churches. One of those who approached me, a man of obvious intelligence and good education, voiced an almost violent antipathy to the use of manuscripts in preaching. It seemed clear to him that written sermons constitute the most debilitating influence in the life of the churches in this century.

When I ventured to suggest that perhaps he was really objecting to poorly written manuscripts, that closer attention by ministers to an oral style and vigorous reading might change his mind, he dismissed the idea abruptly. "Not at all," he said, "it's the principle of the thing that I object to. When a person who has been trained in theology has to write out sermons he is saying that the Christian faith is too complicated to be preached from the heart. And I don't buy that at all. The gospel is simple. And it should be kept that way!"

"The gospel is simple." That statement expresses one of the most popular, plausible, and thoroughly demoralizing opinions about Christian faith.

There are obviously some short declarative sentences taken from the Bible by which significantly descriptive things can be said about the gospel. The most familiar and beloved of them is perhaps, "God was in Christ reconciling the world unto himself." But to imagine that having said this is to have presented the listener with a useful, relevant condensation of all truth necessary to salvation is errant nonsense. One can hear Wordsworth's definition of poetry as "emo-

23

tion recollected in tranquility" or Shakespeare's description of acting as holding "the mirror up to nature" without becoming either a poet or an actor. Nor would any sane person state the formula for nuclear fission and suppose that he or she had thereby explained the lifework of Albert Einstein. Formulas of that kind may be useful to stir imagination or activate minds already disciplined in a particular field. But they can in no way take the place of the arduous thought which must lie at the heart of all true understanding.

Something of this infirmity afflicts all simple summaries of Christian faith. They leave unanswered, indeed unaddressed, a host of questions which human beings are forced to confront every day as they struggle to cope with the challenges and opportunities hurled at them by life, questions by which the individual's self-perceptions are significantly influenced.

Many of the resounding slogans of piety, biblical and traditional, which comfort the intellectually lazy and furnish preachers with ringing conclusions for their sermons are virtually meaningless. They are like those easy-to-assemble do-it-yourself kits which, when one gets them home, turn out to require tools and skills that no one in the family possesses.

Now I realize that I must pause at this point for a very important explanatory note. It would be natural in the light of what I have just said to assume that the chief agent of Christian oversimplification is the pastor, the man or woman in the pulpit eager to reach untutored minds. And surely some of the blame does fall on those shoulders. But before we can even reach an arraignment of the ministry for this offense, there is an important confession to be elicited from the academy.

There is a kind of perverse Christian humility which sometimes leads even very distinguished and sophisticated scholars to pay devout lip service to the simplistic tradition, which encourages men and women who have devoted their lives to the study of texts and systems of thought to declare publicly, when the circumstances are right, that their hard-won and cherished wisdom is as dross when compared to the golden insights of semiliterate piety.

I would almost rather have my right hand wither than write this. But the late, very great Reinhold Niebuhr, standing in the pulpit of Marquand Chapel for his Lyman Beecher Lectures in 1945, paused in the middle of one of his anguished periods, looked reflectively out the window and interjected, "You know, sometimes I think that the little old lady with the Bible open in her lap understands these things better than we do with all our elaborate structures of analysis and ratiocination."

And how can we forget the infamous response of Karl Barth, who when asked to sum up his faith in a single sentence, said, "Jesus loves me. This I know; for the Bible tells me so." Whereupon every pulpit-pounding demagogue in the land shouted "Praise the Lord!" and cancelled his subscription to *The Reader's Digest*.

The most charitable thing that can be said of Niebuhr's lapse is that it was sheer hypocrisy. That magnificent mind never for an instant believed that some mysterious, superior wisdom inheres in the undisciplined opinions of people who pride themselves upon their ignorant piety. It is, in fact, of the essence of Niebuhr's contribution to the thought of our time that he insisted upon looking the terrible complexity of creation full in the face.

As for Karl Barth's comment, I am inclined to dismiss it with the words used by a Roman Catholic magazine to acknowledge the death of Sigmund Freud: "His silly ideas fooled many."

In his *Anti-Intellectualism in American Life*, Richard Hofstadter both chronicles the simplistic tendency in American religion and analyses its vulgarization of culture in the United States. He tells, for example, of a Georgia assemblyman who voted against public libraries because all the truth worth knowing is in the Bible.

Hofstadter's charge is well documented by such commentators upon American history as Henry Steele Commager and Max Lerner, who describe in their own ways the impoverishment of human intelligence at the hands of simple religion. Reading the record accumulated by such authors one can understand the wry comment of Nicholas Brown of Providence, Rhode Island, who, when asked why he had given the money to establish a university, replied, "My Baptist faith has done so much to vulgarize the American mind that I feel an obligation to make some recompense."

There is obviously a kind of profound simplicity which lies *beyond* the intellectual struggles of great Christian thinkers and is made possible by those struggles. When a man like Niebuhr says, "God was in Christ reconciling . . . ," every word in that familiar sentence carries a load of meaning accumulated during years of rigorous study, bold thought, and informed experience. And when Karl

Barth elected to ignore John 3:16 in favor of simple lines from a children's hymn he spoke from the massive intellectual background which eventuated in a voluminous flow of obscure prose.

Years ago I attended a concert-lecture by an accomplished teacher of piano. During the discussion period that followed his formal presentation he was asked what he considered the most challenging piece of music ever composed for the piano. To the amusement of the audience he instantly replied, "Chopsticks." But when the laughter had died down, the pianist went on to give a delightful fifteen-minute talk on the ways in which that familiar exercise exemplifies various harmonic devices and technical problems for the performing artist. (In fact, the lecture was so good that I suspect that the question had been planted.)

Now for a skilled musician to do that kind of thing is a permissible gimmick, a personal tour de force. But no one in his or her right mind would allow a ten-year-old child to abandon practice of the piano on the ground that having mastered "Chopsticks" he or she had taken command of the most significant work ever composed for the instrument. It is obviously one thing to appreciate "Chopsticks" *beyond* Chopin, let us say, and quite another thing to appreciate "Chopsticks" *this side* of Liberace.

Now I should be the first to admit that simplicity and complexity are highly relative terms. What might be a painfully simple lecture in chemistry, for example, for people educated in the science would be a nightmare of complexity for me. There are millions of men and women in the world who lack the educational or intellectual basis for dealing with Christian theology at any but the most elementary level. They have a right to be addressed where they live and in language which reaches their hearts and minds.

But there is a vast difference between simplification as a *pedagogical method*, as a concession to the limitations of the audience, and similar simplification represented as a sacred, God-given substitute for informed understanding. It is one thing to meet people where they are and help them in the journey toward wisdom. It is quite another thing to assure the same people that the journey is wholly unnecessary—and may, indeed, reflect a state of spiritual disease.

It is, I will argue, grotesquely irresponsible for scholars whose comments represent inherent intelligence, decades of disciplined study, and the outermost reaches of painful imagination to imply that what they have so hardly come by can be had cut-rate by semilit-

26

erate piety, no matter how sincere that piety may be. For playing to the groundlings in this matter, academic theologians must acknowledge a substantial burden of guilt.

The biblical faith is finally complex because the God to whom it bears witness is veiled in mystery. And the efforts of finite creatures to relate to that God inevitably bring them face to face with this awesome fact. It is, therefore, the first responsibility of preaching to engage men and women in a search which is the very essence of human existence in history, not a mere prelude to its successful appropriation.

This painful truth is spelled out on almost every page of the Bible. It appears first and most explicitly, of course, in the Book of Genesis. Adam and Eve are shown there living in a state of complete rapport with both their Creator and their environment. They enjoy what has been called "an instinctive knowledge of God." Or, as some theologians prefer to put it, they relate to the divine at the unconscious levels of the mind. They can do what comes naturally, serene in the confidence that it will be pleasing or, as we say today, "acceptable" to the Most High.

When, however, the man and woman seize the power to distinguish between good and evil they lose their spontaneous rapport with God and are driven out of Eden. Now it is vitally important for what I want to say here about the complexity of the biblical faith to note well the double nature of the consequences of their action, their punishment. Adam and Eve might have been stripped of their instinctive or unconscious sense of the divine will but allowed to remain in the garden. Had that been the case, had they been required to exercise their new-found ability to choose *within* the context of God's immediate presence, which is the character of Eden, they might by the responsible and disciplined use of their power have retained something approximating their original rapport with the Eternal. The environmental conditions, one might say, for formal obedience would have continued to exist. Or to put it another way, only a single variable would have been introduced into the theological equation. Perfect decisions and their presumably blissful consequences would, in theory at least, have remained possible.

But the Bible tells us that the man and woman are not allowed to remain in Eden. They are expelled into the world to exercise their ability to choose in a new and radically different context, one in which the face of God is forever veiled and the divine will known only in fragments and snatches, in visions and dreams. Imperfect knowledge of the truth is not merely an incidental attribute of life in history. It is the very essence of life in history. It is what makes history what it is.

The Old Testament declares this plainly in many ways, most dramatically, perhaps, in the Book of Exodus in which Moses is told in so many words that no mortal being can look upon the face of God and live. Now unless we assume that Yahweh like the Wizard of Oz must remain hidden because the reality is so much less impressive than the facade, the voice so much more beautiful than the countenance, God's warning to Moses in this encounter must be intended not to protect the sanctity of the divine—but to preserve the humanity of the human.

God knows that no finite creature can look directly upon the face of the ultimate, transcendent reality and continue to take seriously those equivocal causes and painful choices that are essential to human existence. The power to choose between good and evil, that most majestic, definitive attribute of human beings in the Bible, has significance only where truth is veiled and the answer to every question shrouded in uncertainty.

What the Old Testament describes in story form is verified every day in the relationships of life, so much so that the distinguished physician-philosopher, Lewis Thomas, has recently written that human beings "have been selected in evolution for the gift of ambiguity. . . . Uncertainty, the sure sense that the ground is shifting at every step, is one of the marks of humanity."

The relationship between this inherent "uncertainty" and the freedom of the race is inescapable. No one derives satisfaction or gets much credit for solving arithmetic problems whose answers are already written on the blackboard. Nor do we hail a person's judgment of horseflesh for predicting the winner of last year's Kentucky Derby. Choice and decision have meaning only when one cannot know with absolute certainty which of two or more possibilities will be the most rewarding. Human beings are compelled to choose. But they must always do so in terms of an understanding that is at best partial. They are required to judge. But they can never be certain even in retrospect of the rightness of their judgments.

This state of affairs makes life a painful business, one that fills the hearts and minds of men and women with deep frustration. The only thing about which we can be sure is that our best efforts to understand God's will fully are inevitably inadequate because we have been "driven away from the face of the Lord."

Here, then, is the fundamental human predicament. In order to affirm our particular existence apart from the all-embracing unity of the divine, we become creatures of choice, bundles of individuation, and thus fragment the cosmos in our own minds. And in order to be really free we must be to some degree separated and insulated from the immediate presence of truth of every kind. Now we see "in a glass darkly" and know only "in part."

Most people experience the relevance of this hard reality in their parental roles. In the raising of children it is never possible to give freedom as a gift. It must always, by its very nature, be seized. How futile and foolish it would be for Mother and Father to encourage their offspring to stand up for their own rights in various domestic contretemps. ("That's right, call Daddy nasty names!") To defy authority simply because one has been exhorted by authority to do so is no real exercise of personal identity at all. It is, as millions of Chinese discovered in their Cultural Revolution, just another, somewhat more subtle, form of subservience.

More often than not most parents discover eventually that the emergence of an authentic human personality is not some gentle parlor game that any number can play without damage to the furniture. It is the extension of that process of individuation that began at the dawn of time. And it is always painful for everyone involved. If anything can give some comfort to the family of mutinous adolescents, it may be the realization that what is breaking up the household is neither mere accident nor the consequence of some tactical parental failure, but a process both elemental and inevitable.

Just as children must assert themselves and their freedom by decisions which can be injurious to themselves and those they love, so human beings in general are compelled to affirm the particularities of their humanity against the absolute power of God, that power in which time, place, and personality cease to exist. For me this is the real substance of the doctrine of original sin. It is neither that our worst is so bad nor that our best is always so inadequate. It is the tragic fact that our best is always to some degree the fruit of our rebellion against the divine Absolute. True humanity was not, as some suggest, defaced by the Fall. It was made possible by the Fall.

Most people who are not professionally committed to believe otherwise, that is to say, lay men and women, understand this awesome fact of life. And in spite of the frequency with which they consent to sing and pray about the joy of being reunited with the *transcendent* love of God, they give little evidence of really wanting to escape the confusing challenges, equivocal values, and agonizing decisions that make up life in history.

At some level of consciousness even simplistically pious men and women understand that their human nature, with all that is good and bad in it, depends to some degree upon separation from the Absolute. They sense that their manhood and womanhood are intimately linked, essentially expressed within the particular relativities of their daily lives, that finitude is the character rather than the disfigurement of their humanity.

There is an old homiletic chestnut that expresses this feeling well. It concerns a rip-snorting preacher who set out one Sunday morning to portray the joys of heaven in such glowing terms that the congregation would become eager to go there at all costs in immediate carnal gratifications. After sermonizing for a while he asked dramatically, "How many of you, Brothers and Sisters, want to go to Heaven?" All but one member of the flock raised their hands.

So the preacher labored on, determined to leave no soul in darkness. Then he asked again, "Now how many of you want to go to Heaven?" Once more every hand but one was raised.

Troubled by the recalcitrance of this single sinner, the pastor finished up the service quickly and hastened down into the pews for some personal evangelism.

"My friend," he asked earnestly, "don't you want to go to Heaven when you die?"

The recalcitrant's face cleared, and he gave a great sigh of relief. "Oh, sure, Reverend," he said, "I want to go to Heaven *when I die*. But from the way you was carryin' on I figured you was gettin' up a party to leave right away."

The significance of this anecdote lies not in its content per se, although it does make my point, but in its widespread acceptance among people whom most of us would regard as fundamentalists, adherents of a doggedly other-worldly pietism. I have heard the story told several times by radio and television preachers at revival-type services. And in each instance the audience reacted with the roar of spontaneous, slightly embarrassed laughter by which people reveal that some supposedly secret weakness or vice of their own has been uncovered—the laughter which says, in effect, "What a relief to discover that I am not the only one who does that!" This is the response which people of my generation used to have to jokes about the lusts of the flesh.

That reaction is important, because it reveals the audience's real reservations about the theology which it professes in religious terms and in more guarded moments. As vigorously as they would deny it in Bible class on Sunday, even very conservative Christians acknowledge in subtle ways that this world is in an important sense their home, because it is the place which makes possible the contingent existence by which *human* being is defined.

Lest it be suspected that this feeling is confined to unsophisticated laity with little learning in the subtleties of the faith, one of this century's greatest theologians confided in conversation that heaven would not be truly heaven for him, unless he could continue his theological research there.

Ponder for a moment the implications of that statement. I take it that theology has to do with the study of God and God's will for human beings. Thus, my learned friend was saying that *even in heaven* there could be no real fulfillment for him, unless there remained sufficient separation between the divine and the human to give meaning to research.

If it is possible for a devout and theologically sophisticated person to regard some imperishable attribute of human being as requiring a degree of separation from the Eternal even in heaven, how much more essential must some such separation seem for the preservation of life in history.

What most of us realize when we are not playing religious games is that much of the richness of life lies in those unique configurations which make each of us different from every other. And we understand, if only instinctively, that this particularity is a by-product of our finitude.

I love my wife and children, for example, *not* as manifestations of being in general, but as specific, eccentric individuals. And I hope they love me the same way. The qualities that make people lovable are those which distinguish and separate. What we call "personality" is our fragmentary character, the jagged outlines of our uniqueness. What attracts us to other men and women is that which makes them stand out, not that which makes them blend into the human mass.

It is an acceptance of this fact that constitutes one of the major ways in which biblical faith differs from the great religions of the East. And our failure as preachers to appreciate and explore this fact does as much to devitalize Christian proclamation as any other single factor.

My wife and I once spent a weekend on Martha's Vineyard and we picked up a young man who was hitchhiking along one of the island's more remote roads. In an effort to initiate conversation my wife expressed gratification that the weather that day was clear and sunny, something that is not often the case on the Vineyard.

The young fellow turned on her a blank, unfocused gaze and replied, "I like rain and fog, too. Rain and fog are beautiful."

Mrs. Muehl readily agreed that each mood of nature has its own charms, but allowed as how for an afternoon of swimming, fishing, and sailing she preferred sunshine.

To this our passenger responded, in his dull monotone, "I don't *prefer* anything. Everything is beautiful to me. I take it all as it comes along."

Well, it was obvious that our friend was into some cultic commitment to reunify the cosmos by denying distinctions among the phenomena that he encountered daily. (He was also into some heavy grass!) And he was not going to let two middle-aged squares disrupt his karma with talk about good weather and bad. And in the flatness of his voice, the blank face, and empty eyes there was a vivid illustration of what one finds again and again in those who seek to escape the fragmentation of the human condition by denying its reality. His whole manner suggested that in disdaining to focus upon anything in particular he expected to view the eternal, that by pretending to have no preferences he could achieve unity with pure being. And in the process he seemed, to us at least, to have thoroughly dehumanized himself.

In somewhat more subtle form Christians often exhibit the same tendency. I knew a clergyman once who, under the spell of a radical commitment to the gospel, was so determined to love everybody the same that he actually loved nobody at all. In the manner of a professional religious diplomat he greeted all with the same bland smile, the same slight bow, the same carefully measured cordiality and routine inquiries about home and hearth. One scarcely felt identified by him, much less cared about in any special way. And in the eyes of this man's wife and children one could see the bright tracings of frost on a winter windowpane.

While the mystic tries to withdraw from history and lose himself or herself to some degree in the featurelessness of the Eternal, most of us choose another way. We seek to ease the tension that is life by concretizing God in some tangible and manageable fashion. And it is this concretizing of the divine, this effort to consolidate God's self-disclosures that constitutes the essential element of what we call idolatry.

It is incorrect, I am persuaded, to believe as many do today that the problem of idolatry is the tendency to identify the *wrong* thing as God. That is, we make a god of money or power or sex or status and so on. The crux of the problem is *not*, I suggest, the identification of the *wrong* thing as God, but the very process of attempting to identify the divine in particular terms, the effort to cram the massively complex nature of the Most High into some single principle of interpretation.

That, I suppose, was what really lay at the heart of even the most sophisticated Jew's refusal to carve statues or paint pictures of the Lord. It was not simply that ignorant people might bow down and worship the image. The real problem was that even quite intelligent people might be tempted by this act of portrayal to suppose that God *can be* so unified and harmonized in human terms, that some such depiction is possible.

So long as we have only what might be called mental perceptions of the divine, there is room to accommodate the paradoxes of revelation. But as soon as one begins to draw pictures, one has to resolve many paradoxes and make the sorts of decisions which dispel the ambiguities characteristic of God's presence in history. So Israel was forbidden to portray the Almighty not because it might be tempted to fall on its knees before an image nor because it might make some insulting mistake about the details of the divine features. No, it was because the very act of portraying assumes that it is possible to pull together the contradictory manifestations of the Eternal and resolve the paradoxes inherent in revelation. It is the effort to rationalize God that is the essence of idolatry.

What this means, of course, is that the sin in idolatry is much more subtle and insidious than most of us suppose. It is present in our misplaced loyalties and affections, our devotion to money, power, reputation, sex, and so on. It does often appear in that chauvinism which exalts one's nation or race above every other value. But these are in a sense its more obvious and less destructive disguises.

Far more potent and dangerous is the ability of idolatry to present itself as one or another form of piety. It may appear in the assumption that God can be encapsulated in sincerity. ("Just do your best. That's all that counts.") Sometimes it takes the form of devotion to the Bible, the assumption that God has been made the prisoner of Scripture and can only be known in the modes of appearance revealed there. And often well-meaning people try to pack all of the Eternal into their image of Jesus of Nazareth, asking in life's crises what the Lord would have done, as though this counsel opens the floodgates of wisdom about the divine will.

False gods always fail and fall, however. Every effort to reduce God to simplicity, every effort to capture the divine essence in those pious generalizations that fit so well on bumper stickers, every honest and dishonest subversion of the paradoxes inherent in revelation ultimately betrays us. And we are compelled to recognize that the divine complexity shatters all attempts to simplify truth. The core of Christian faith is not blessed assurance but the willingness to live and wrestle with the terrifying uncertainty that is our freedom.

What I am saying, you see, is that the human commitment to the particular in both personality and experience, the deep need to define existence over against the Absolute in ways that are both exclusive and excluding can make a tragedy of simple faith. For such a faith inevitably tries to interpret a multidimensional human experience in terms of a two-dimensional piety. It seeks not so much to cope with the tension that is life as to resolve or transcend it. And in so doing it risks the subversion of human nature. Devout men and women are encouraged to believe that large areas of their lives are quite irrelevant to the divine purpose or even actually repugnant to it. And salvation becomes too often a process of self-mutilation, an effort to make one's self small enough to fit into the mind of God.

It is a fundamental responsibility of the preacher as theologian to resist the illusory charms of the simple gospel. In the chapters that follow I want to sketch something of what this means for me. But before all else, it implies an end to our grievous neglect and frequent denigration of intelligence in the life of faith. Arthur Schopenhauer once said that all religions offer rewards for excellence of the heart and emotions, but no religion offers rewards for excellence of the mind and understanding. That may not hit the mark squarely, but it comes too close to Christianity for comfort.

I cite this as the special responsibility of the preacher-theologian, because it is in the sermon that the sequence of intellectual activity that moves the minister from school to college to seminary is most often broken, and the distinction between profound simplicity and vulgar simplification is lost.

Whatever academic theologians may *say* about the virtues of the heart and emotions as expressions of piety, they are enabled, indeed, required by their jobs to use their intellects regularly and in stimulating relation to their faith. In the process of being theologians, ethicists, biblical scholars, and Christian educators they are called upon to use their minds as tools of Christian perception; and thus they derive those gratifications and enrichments of personality which intellectual engagement with the faith affords.

Often, however, this commendable intellectual vitality is not inspired by preaching, is, indeed, discouraged by both ratio descidendi and dicta, that is, by both doctrinal formulation and incidental comment. An insidious kind of clericalism suggests that there is a qualitative difference between priest and people where excellences of the mind and understanding are concerned. The power to choose responsibly, which constitutes such an essential feature of our human being, is too often treated by the pulpit as a mere expression of character, something which is validated, if at all, by the good faith with which it is exercised.

Too many sermons treat the human mind as a secondary instrumentality or as merely the means by which believers express their gratitude to God for the gift of omnipotent grace, rather than as a significant part of the way in which grace is recognized and appropriated. And as a result, "the little old lady with the Bible open in her lap" continues to haunt the household of faith, frightening away the young.

In some ways those of us who teach in seminaries remind one of Phyllis Schlafly. She travels around the country being honored at all kinds of gatherings, speaks before large audiences, dines with the great and near great, and appears on television talk shows, all in order to tell women to stay home and mind the house. Too many of us who earn our livings and get our psychological brownie points from thinking deeply about religion can be heard to counsel others that a warm heart is better than an active mind in matters of faith.

If practical proof of the seriousness of this problem is needed, a good bit is available in the terrible collapse of Christian education in the American churches. Once flourishing Sunday schools have been reduced to baby-sitting operations in many communities. Recruiting teachers is a little like signing up volunteers for an experiment with the bubonic plague. And, as often as not, where some substantive Christian education program is in place, it stops at the age of twelve, the point at which children are beginning to get some mature notion of what religion is all about.

As for adult education, "discomfort guides my tongue and bids me speak of nothing but despair." In my peripatetic ministry over the past forty years I have had a chance to make an exhaustive, if unscientific, survey of this field. And aside from the ubiquitous Bible study classes in which the pastor confides to a few loyal souls the latest wisdom from the Black Forest, very little is going on worthy of the name education.

When my wife and I were expecting our first child we discovered that no church in our area, despite the rich endowment of theological resources available, had ever undertaken any program to help young people prepare as Christians for the critically important business of becoming parents. Spurred on by that experience, I have asked in scores of churches all over the country whether anyone present in my audience has ever encountered some effort to meet this need. In forty years of putting the query to literally hundreds of people I have encountered only three who could answer in the affirmative. One woman had been in such a class a few decades before, and two others had heard of one from someone else.

It sometimes puzzles me that we are able without embarrassment to speak of the Christian faith as a living power in our lives, something by which we are guided from day to day in all of our relationships, and then do so little to discharge the responsibility which that affirmation implies.

I am sure that there are many reasons for the poverty of our efforts in this respect. There are undoubtedly organizational problems in an increasingly mobile society, problems which complicate the establishment of effective education in the churches. But underlying the whole sad business is the Christian indifference to the life of the mind of which I have been speaking. If professing Christians cannot be persuaded to participate in adult education programs as students or teachers, the fact probably reflects their life-long conviction that learning has no significant place in the work of God. If we are saved by grace alone, what does one need to know beyond that single fact? Simple faith makes a mockery of the educational enterprise.

If a world on the brink of self-destruction pays little heed to religious counsels, that fact may say less about the wickedness of the world than it does about the failure of Christian preaching to interpret the human situation in ways that make sense to thoughtful men and women. Many aspects of the church's present irrelevance probably demand changes in the forms of seminary education. But none of these will avail unless and until preachers claim their proper role as creative theologians and begin to work thoughtfully with the complex dimensions of human experience, not by exhorting their congregations to read scholarly tomes or to simply participate more frequently in Bible study, but by helping people to see the depth and meaning of the mundane, the true profundity of what may appear at first glance to be secular superficiality. Effective homiletic theology consists *not* in making Christian doctrine simple, but in exploring the rich complexity of the lives which it seeks to inform. And in all our preaching it is important to remember that the ability of God to save the most ignorant measures the omnipotence of God, not the value of ignorance.

A story that comes down to us from the tradition of our Jewish forebears in the faith sums up several of the points made in this chapter.

When Adam and Eve were expelled from Eden, the narrative goes, they wasted no time in blaming themselves. Instead, they blamed one another, thus establishing the pattern for married life through the ages. For a time they considered trying to sneak back into Eden. But the gate looked forbidding and the angel with the flaming sword appeared incorruptible. So, with many a backward glance, the man and woman began their journey over the face of the earth, looking for a place to dwell.

Some lands were too hot, others too cold. This place was a desert, that one a swamp. A few that looked and felt just right proved to be shared by large carnivores whose urgent appetites threatened life and limb. The long days of searching dragged painfully into years.

At last Adam and his wife came to a large fertile valley. Sweet grasses grew abundantly in it, and a clear fresh stream ran sparkling through its middle. Gentle herbivorous animals grazed quietly, and fish leaped shining into the sunlight. Far up in one of the valley walls there was a clean, dry cave, with an apron that caught the first rays of the dawn. Here the man and woman settled down.

Things went well for them. Adam tilled the ground and hunted for game. Eve prepared the food, sewed clothing, and grew great with child. Oh, it wasn't Eden. The night a skunk got into the butter crock Eve wept and remembered the garden. The day his plow broke on a large rock Adam cursed and reminded his wife about the apple.

But then one night in spring, when the air was soft and fragrant with the scent of new growth, Adam lay on the apron of the cave, unable to sleep. The sky above him was splashed with stars, the muted lowing of the herds came faintly from the pastures below. Every muscle in the man's body ached from the labors of the day.

Suddenly, Adam turned to his wife.

"Eve, God was wrong! This is what we were meant for. To till the ground and raise our grain. To hunt and fish for meat, to work all day in the hot sun and feel the sweat drying on our bodies in the cool of the evening. To try something and fail and try it again and fail. And keep on trying until it works. To struggle to understand things that fill us with fear. To feel hunger and thirst and pain—and hope! This is better than Eden, Eve. This is what we were meant for. God was wrong, Eve. God was wrong!"

And, the story ends, somewhere so far away that the human mind cannot even imagine the distance and so near that the breath of Adam's speaking was hot against his hand, God heard the words of defiance flung by the man into the deep well of space. And hearing, God smiled.

# CHAPTER 3

# Proclaiming God the Creator

For a few years during the late forties I served as debate coach for a local chapter of the American Institute of Banking. This was the period in which banks were beginning to shed the deeply conservative image that had been characteristic of them in the past. The new spirit of openness generated some unexpected attitudes. And one of them was the eagerness of our debaters to tackle a great range of topics, some of which raised economic, social, and political issues that had previously been anathema in banking circles. In our postdebate discussions over coffee the spirit of liberation persisted. And the conversation roamed over areas of controversy only remotely related to the subject of the evening. The minds of these men and women had been turned loose to think the unthinkable.

Following a heated argument about the nature and destiny of capitalism (more bankers have serious questions about this than one might expect) a middle-aged trust officer, a pillar of his church, waited for me at the elevator after class with a problem on his mind.

"You know, Doc," he said, "I've always thought of myself as a religious man, and I take some kidding from friends about my church activities. But tonight when we were discussing some of the ethical problems of capitalism I suddenly realized that if I ever had to choose between capitalism and Christianity, I'd stick with capitalism. Am I going to Hell?"

I put on my best Rogerian manner, which is none too good, and in the few minutes available to us I tried to suggest some of the implications of his question. It was obviously bothering him seriously and was not merely a debating ploy. And in the course of our conversation I began to understand some of the difficulties which traditional Christian preaching can present to men and women for whom religion is an aspect of life, not a full-time preoccupation.

You see, my banker friend was not expressing some grossly materialistic determination to accumulate great riches at all costs, even his hope of heaven. He was a man of limited means, and it was obvious to us both that his future held in store little more than another decade or so of anonymous service at a modest salary. His commitment to capitalism reflected no mere addiction to money per se. It sprang, rather, from an almost inarticulate, scarcely identified but deeply rooted feeling about human creativity in general and his own reason for being in particular.

The banker was saying that if he ever had to choose between what he had been taught by preachers to regard as Christian ethical precepts and participation in a creative process, which for him was economic, he would be inclined to go with the latter. He felt a *need* to be creative, a need which clearly outweighed his obviously sincere commitment to Christian faith, as he understood it. And he clearly feared that the two might be incompatible.

It should not be hard to understand the source of the man's uneasiness. Traditional preaching, especially in its Protestant forms, has little to say about human creativity. It talks somewhat about justice and a great deal about mercy as attributes of Christian character and to varying degrees exhorts believers to value those virtues. But for the most part it seems willing to leave all forms of initiation to impulses for which it can find little place in the lexicon of spiritual values.

My favorite illustration of this attitude is a story that comes down to us from the Middle Ages. It is about an eloquent monk who was justly famous for his preaching and went about the countryside addressing all sorts and conditions of human beings. He spoke on many topics, but after the manner of preachers he had his favorite. It was the beauty of the celibate life. And to this subject he brought the full power of his rhetorical gifts.

One day when the spirit had been poured out with a special generosity he was approached by a lusty peasant lad who had been an attentive member of his audience.

"Brother," the young man said, "I was much moved by your words and almost persuaded. But one thing bothers me. If all people felt as you do, what would become of the human race?"

The old monk smiled wryly and answered, "My young friend, you need have no fear on that score. There will always be enough unbridled carnality abroad to populate even so vast a realm as this earth."

There we have it boldly stated: the feeling that some aspects of human behavior which are indispensable to the survival of the race can be excluded from our definition of Christian personality, along with a willingness to consign the most elemental energies of life to sinful, even demonic, vitalities, an attitude expressed only somewhat more moderately by C. S. Lewis when he said that while human creativity "may be innocent," it is surely not "important."

This problem has in the past been reflected most visibly in the realm of human sexuality. And I feel sure that many of the painful dilemmas that confront us there today spring from the ambivalence about creativity of which I am speaking. But as my banker friend perceived, the tendency influences other areas of life as well.

At a conference on stewardship a few years ago one of the prominent businessmen present sat through several hours of discussion in stony silence. Then he finally burst out, "Why do I always get the feeling from preachers that the only Christian thing to do with my business is to sell it and divide the proceeds among the poor?"

The man was obviously overreacting to the tone of the theological statements that had been read. But to some degree I could sympathize with him. Human vitalities have been too often treated by the pulpit as more of a problem than an asset.

My own consciousness in this matter was raised recently by an incident that occurred in one of our preaching classes. For some years now we have been having our students in the introductory courses listen to a taped sermon by Dr. Norman Vincent Peale. The purpose of this exercise is not to commend Dr. Peale's theology but to demonstrate how simple, direct, and profusely illustrated a sermon can be without insulting the intelligence of the congregation. Whatever else one might want to say about Dr. Peale's preaching, it is obviously listened to eagerly by people of many backgrounds and levels of education.

When the tape ends students have until recently been quick to point out that the congregations at the Marble Collegiate Church are made up of the world's achievers, people of an upwardly mobile orientation. And this observation has been made in tensely critical tones.

But on this occasion one of the young men in the class listened to these remarks, and then he said, "You know, I sometimes think that the world's *achievers* may be the most neglected people in our churches today."

Well, as you can imagine, his classmates jumped all over him. Was he not aware, they demanded to know, that our churches are *run* by their affluent members, that denominational boards and councils are made up of the movers and shakers in the community?

"Oh, I realize that the achievers *govern* the institution," the student at bay replied. "But I wonder how many of them feel helpfully addressed by our preaching. How much real understanding of *their* problems do we show? What do we offer as an alternative to positive thinking?"

What alternative do most of us offer the so-called *achievers* in the congregation to the onward and upward theology which they obviously find so attractive? For that matter, do we even understand *why* that theology appeals as strongly as it does to so many men and women? And is it not possible that our interpretations of the phenomenon are every bit as superficial as the gospel that we criticize?

I have become persuaded that there are a great many people like my banker friend in our churches today, men and women whose *apparent* addiction to economic and social advancement reflects *not* crass materialism but an often unguided, uninformed urge to express *creative* energies at work within them, energies which traditional preaching does little or nothing to help them understand and harness responsibly. Like caged squirrels they run endlessly on little treadmills in an effort to discharge the restlessness inherent in their human natures. And all that many of us do in our sermons is cluck our tongues critically at so much frantic getting and spending.

Nicolai Berdyaev once said that the *negative* aspect of Christian morality is self-discipline; the *positive* aspect of that morality is commitment to a greatly creative task. Purposeful movement, he argues, may do more to help people keep their moral balance than a grim determination to be righteous or gratitude to God for their salvation.

I want to argue here that the tendency of Christian preaching to concentrate upon justice and mercy as expressions of faith to the virtual exclusion of authentic creativity causes that preaching to neglect significant areas of human potential *and* leave unemployed effective tools for the healing of both individuals and communities. There are critical problems facing human beings which cannot be solved by the mere well-meaning rearrangement of their component

elements, problems which require, rather, a challenge to those inge-
nuities inherent in the race.

Joseph Sittler put this well when he said that men and women
should not be "reduced by religion to their own interior dimensions." Surely one form of such reductionism is the effort so common in the pulpit to proclaim the gospel without reference to those
creative energies that break down walls, push back boundaries, force
redefinitions, and open new vistas to imagination.

I once heard a psychiatrist speak of a patient who could not force
herself to get out of bed in the morning until she had planned in
detail a schedule for the entire day ahead of her. She believed, said
the therapist, that reality could be controlled by the proper arrangement of interior data. The result was that she never *did* get out of
bed, until some external urgency forced her to do so.

Much preaching tends to encourage something of this inertia
in Christians. It exhorts them to keep examining and rearranging
their interior decor rather than reach out for those new experiences
that might enlarge the dimensions of their personalities. This has always been a temptation for preachers, and it is becoming even
more respectable with the current enthusiasm for something called
"spirituality."

Now it is easy to overlook the interiorization of our message
because so much social gospel emphasis does, indeed, draw the individual out of himself or herself in concern for the needs of others.
And I do not for one moment want to denigrate that important
response to preaching. But all too often the content of what we like
to call the "prophetic" word is a summons to the public rearrangement of the furniture which simulates creativity more than it stimu-
lates it. Congregations are exhorted to change their priorities rather
than expand their perspectives, to sacrifice some of their pie, as it
were, so that others may enjoy somewhat larger shares. And the
reward offered for such self-denial is very often the sense of an oner-
ous duty well done rather than an enriched and deepened experience of God at work in history.

This is what I mean when I say that the failure to challenge human
creativity and give it an honorable place in our proclamation
deprives preaching of an effective tool for individual and social reformation. There are multitudes of people both in and out of our
churches who resist a commitment which seems to them to be a kind

of self-mutilation, people who might respond and respond *sacrificially* to a challenge which drew upon and enlarged their creative potential.

It is unfortunate, I am persuaded, that in its understandable attempts to escape the ethos of works righteousness, contemporary preaching underestimates the redemptive possibilities in work. Even sophisticated members of the clergy are inclined toward what I think of as a magical interpretation of divine mercy. That is, they often treat God's compassion as something which descends mysteriously from above in "the still dews of quietness" to transform the lives of sinners in a manner which appears to have little if any historical data in it. Far too little is said in most sermons about the substance of new being in everyday life. The result of this omission drains much of the dignity from existence and generates endless uncertainty about the content of the Christian witness beyond the confines of the church itself.

Many years ago I attended a testimonial dinner honoring a man who had spent his life in campus ministry. For almost half a century he had served colleges and universities and played an important, if quiet, part in shaping modern educational policy.

In the course of the evening predictable speeches were given praising the guest of honor for his great effectiveness in dealing with students. And a couple of the speakers referred to the number of young people who had gone off to college intending to be doctors, lawyers, architects, scientists, or something of the sort, but who, after association with the chaplain, had changed their career plans and gone into the ministry.

What a splendid thing, these speakers declaimed, to have worked such redemptive miracles in the lives of the young.

At the end of the evening I walked back to the campus with the subject of these encomiums and found him strangely depressed. The hour was late, and I assumed that he was feeling both tired and a bit down about this formal close of his career. But when I ventured to say so he brushed my explanation aside and said, "I have spent my life trying to show young people how they can serve God in whatever they feel called to do. It hurts to be reminded at this late date just how many of them decided to avoid the struggle and take refuge in the nearest pulpit."

The chaplain need not have blamed himself entirely for this situation. The neglect of human creativity in Christian thought has made it difficult, to say the least, to talk persuasively and in any detail about how one lives out the faith in so-called secular vocations. In the face of this ambiguity, the temptation to take refuge in the pulpit—or, to speak confessionally, in a theological seminary faculty—is hard to resist.

My banker friend feared that he might be asked to choose between Christianity and capitalism. The form of his concern may have been naive. Its substance is shared by more and more sincere people in our time. And theological seminaries are enrolling a great many mature men and women who, by their own recognizance, see the ministry as an answer to the dilemma of which I have been speaking.

Archimedes said that he could lift the world if he had a place to rest his lever. Surely we have in our sermons an obligation to suggest, at least, some of the multitudinous points in human experience at which the *divine lever* is known to have rested in lifting fallen men and women. I am persuaded that if we do, we shall find, as Berdyaev suggested, that more of those points than we may at first suspect are moments of commitment to a greatly creative task. And when we fail to do so, when we seem to say that the divine lever rests only on Calvary, we deprive salvation of its historical content, turn ministry into a halfway house and the cross into a magic wand.

Our problem begins, I am convinced, in our christological determination to say everything that needs to be said about God in New Testament terms, in the language of redemption. The magnificent witness of the Old Testament to the God who cannot be subsumed under any single category of human experience, the God who is not fully manifest in any single segment of revelation—the witness of the Old Testament to that complex and terrible reality is tragically muted when we insist, as we so often do, upon treating it as a mere prelude to the really important business transacted at Golgotha and recorded in the Gospels.

When I was confirmed, to get my godmother off my back, that devout Episcopalian gave me two bits of spiritual counsel as the final discharge of the duties she had undertaken at my baptism.

The first was this: Never listen to the Old Testament lesson during Morning Prayer. It will only confuse you.

The second was like unto it: Learn to think of the rector's sermons as a form of penance.

The two are surely not unrelated. An important element in the infirmity of preaching in the apostolic communion is its morbid preoccupation with the Epistles of Paul, which I have always found far more confusing than anything in Genesis or Ecclesiastes.

If one takes the Hebrew Scriptures seriously and regards them as something more than a grace note en route to the Nunc Dimittis, one thing becomes inescapably clear. The God of the Bible is before all else and above all else the Creating One, the one *by whom all things are made* and without whom nothing is made that was made.

And when humanity appears upon the scene it does so as the instrument of that continuing creativity. God's first command, God's defining command to the beings made in the divine image was not that they "let justice roll down like waters and righteousness as a mighty stream." Nor was it that they forgive seventy times seven. It was that they "be fruitful and multiply and fill the earth. . . ."

It was only when Adam and Eve rebelled against being mere reflections of the Absolute, shadows of the divine cast across the ground— it was only then that God was revealed as the Judge. Having chosen the power to choose, humanity was compelled always to choose and became in so doing the instrument of divine judgment.

For me the Old Testament's definition of history is that endless tension established at the dawn of time, the tension between creativity and judgment, energy and form. Humanity is compelled to *act*, to shape and reshape the component elements of being, to dream, imagine, hope, and plan—to push out the boundaries of every moment so that it becomes the future.

But because we are finite, because our best vision is only fragmentary, because the face of truth *is* forever veiled, because we know only in part and understand only in part—all that we create is imperfect and suffers the judgment that perfection, by the very fact of its existence, imposes upon imperfection. For, as Reinhold Niebuhr pointed out, the judgment of God is always partially revealed in the impact of the structures of reality on the vitalities of history which defy those structures.

Small wonder, then, that human beings try so persistently to inhibit God the Creator. We all feel tempted to offer the Eternal a corrupt, self-serving bargain, crying, "If you, O Mighty One, will agree to be somewhat less than fully divine, we will agree to be considerably less than fully human. Let's all go to some quiet corner of the cosmos and play at existence. You be the predictable judge. And we will be your reasonably obedient people. And in that way no one will get hurt too badly."

This is, in a sense, what Israel tried with Torah. To keep God away from the workshop by crowding the docket at the bar. And it has been remarked by commentators in our time that for a people of undoubted vitality and imagination Israel produced a culture painfully lacking in creativity, except in the realm of religion.

For me this is the teaching of the Book of Job. Job was by God's own admission a fully righteous man, scrupulously obeying the Law in all respects. But precisely because of his righteousness, he has come to suppose that God can be defined and controlled by the Law, that God is the Judge only, that Torah has resolved the tension that is history and bound that Most High to one aspect of the divine self-disclosure.

But God will not be a party to this unilateral contract and rejects the limitations which it seeks to impose upon both God and humanity. The Creator cuts with ruthless power across the neatly patterned landscape of Job's juridical piety. And Job cannot understand what has happened. "My *Judge* breaks me without a cause," he cries.

Surely one vivid manifestation of the human denigration of creativity as a spiritual value is found in the trouble that so many people have in making sense of the Book of Job. God does not, as is so often claimed, simply browbeat the man with a display of naked power but lifts Job for a magnificent moment out of the realm of Judgment in which the man has sought to imprison both of them and shows him something of the complex majesty of the Creator.

God's word to Job is shot through with the language of generation and initiation. "Were you there when I laid the foundation of the earth and stretched the line upon it? . . . Who determined its measurements? On what were its bases sunk? Or who laid its cornerstone? Has the rain a father, or who has begotten the drops of dew? Whose womb has given birth to the hoarfrost of heaven?"

God insists that Job see the divine priorities and understand that the restless fingers of the Almighty cannot be bound by his finite need for order. And Job, overawed by what he has been shown, understands that God is the great deficit spender who never pays back but always pays forward by that perpetual inflation of values called "creativity." And Job cries, "I have uttered what I did not understand; things too wonderful for me, which I did not know."

In ways to be discussed in later chapters, we Christians have tried to do with God the Redeemer what Israel tried to do with God the Judge. We seem to be persuaded that creativity has been successfully subordinated to compassion and that the complex majesty of the divine has been crammed willy-nilly into the person of Jesus of Nazareth. Our preaching is saturated with what the late H. Richard Niebuhr called "the Unitarianism of the Second Person." And we, too, reveal in our sermons and in our lives the disfiguring consequence of such presumption. For whenever people try to perform a gentling operation upon the tumultuous God of the Bible they inevitably discover the scars of that same tragic surgery upon their own persons.

There are two basic ways in which we as preachers often fail in our responsibility to proclaim the vital reality of God's continuingly creative love. More often than not we simply say nothing about the subject. For most pulpit purposes the Creator has finished the job and retired to Florida. Divine creativity seldom appears as a contemporary dynamic in history, as something to be dealt with in anything more than what might be called "rhapsodic" terms in the homiletic equation. Spring brings its annual crop of bad poetry about rebirth. And the dedication of the new education wing produces prayers of gratitude for architects and artisans.

But most of these things have a kind of by-the-way retrospective quality to them. We take note of constructive energies at work in our world when their task has been completed. It is almost as though they are fortuitous, random forces in history to which we can relate only in gratitude and awe. Their availability to transform personality and community rarely finds expression in the pulpit.

Even when our preaching does include consideration of God's creating love, however, it seldom suggests its tension with judgment and mercy. That is, creativity is proclaimed as an attribute of God which can be easily and comfortably fitted into the total pattern of a tranquil divine–human relationship. Preachers are inclined to say that God is creative in the way that one might say of a highly intelligent person that he or she is handsome or beautiful, as though the two qualities can and do reside amicably together. What gets lost in this kind of proclamation is an understanding of the inevitable tension that exists between creativity and judgment within the finite realm.

In an uncorrupted world the two would be compatible. But east of Eden where God is encountered always in fragmentary ways and truth is seen only in a glass darkly—in such an existence creativity and judgment will always seem at war with one another. As Teilhard de Chardin points out, every truly creative life demands its victims, those to whom in pursuit of its own special vision and genius it offers something less than justice. Only in that end time when lion and lamb lie down together will the ultimate unity of the two be visible in a fallen world.

Now when we fail to undergird our preaching with an elucidation of this essentially tragic theme, we preach a gospel which falls far short of the deepest human needs. And we do this in several ways.

The first of our failures is explicated in the Book of Job, about which I spoke earlier. So much that afflicts men and women in this life is not a reflection of God's judgment. And it is certainly not defensible as some subtle strategy of compassion. It can be understood, if at all, only in terms of that awesome power which called worlds into being and still underlies all other manifestations of God's nature. The divine zeal to create will not be inhibited by either our comfort or our personal survival in history.

If the divine purpose for humanity is justice, it is obviously very poorly administered. And speaking from this perspective one of Elie Wiesel's characters, a learned rabbi, cries angrily in the face of a pogrom, "On the day of judgement God will have much to answer for!"

If, on the other hand, God's primary concern is works of mercy, honest people must ask *why* this painful mess called history was ever allowed to come into being in the first place.

It is the creative purpose of God, enshrined in the very atoms of our bodies, a purpose which, in order to fulfill itself in time, must cut ruthlessly across every finite value; it is only this creating purpose that can nerve us to live with some measure of joy even in the midst of suffering.

C. S. Lewis put it plainly when he said, "I would rather believe my suffering to be punishment than to believe that it is without purpose." And those who deal daily with men and women who are suffering greatly know that what enables them to go on is not some vague, mystical faith in a spiritual ambiguity called "divine love," but a deeply planted confidence in the meaning of human experience.

Too often in our preaching we let theology blind us to sound psychology. In our efforts to magnify divine grace and glorify the autonomy of God we destroy the very foundations on which we must stand to interpret the turbulence of daily life, a turbulence which is far more universally characteristic of human existence than the "peace which passes all understanding." No less articulate and dedicated a champion of grace than Martin Luther wrote on one occasion, "He who hears the commandments of God will not be greatly moved. But he who hears the voice of God commanding, how can he fail to be moved by majesty so great?"

Creativity is "the voice of God commanding." When men and women seek to rearrange the component elements of existence, to bring into being that which did not exist before, they become echoes of that word which went forth in the beginning. To help them understand that, to enable them to feel what it means to be co-workers with God, is one of the primary tasks of preaching and gives far more credibility to assurances of divine love in the face of pain than all our bland talk about "gentle Jesus meek and mild."

The second infirmity of preaching which fails to proclaim the continuing creativity of God is that it deprives the faith of one of its most effective means of consolidating and commending human community. For while it is surely true that the creative life demands its victims, it also demands its partners and suppliers.

It is easy to lose sight of this fact because of the tendency in almost every recent generation to romanticize the creative rebel, the person whose peculiar genius can best or only be expressed in separation, even isolation, from the human mass. The late Ayn Rand in much of her fiction extols the alienated virtuoso who neither wants nor needs any helpers on the way to his or her private perfection. And there is a school of art which obviously puts such a premium upon self-expression that only the artist and a few precocious souls privy to his or her psychic trauma can make sense of what has been created.

But far more often the creative act gathers rather than disperses community. Artists and artisans are dependent upon the support and assistance of others in ways that most of them understand only too well. What the architect dreams remains only an incomplete dream, until he or she is able to recruit the gifts of others in its realization. One can demean this reality by calling it the use of one human being by another. But that is simply to put an unjustified value judgment upon a significant aspect of God's way of working. Of course we use one another in the fulfillment of the visions that haunt and motivate our lives. But there are more and less responsible ways of doing so. And often the process of incorporating others into our most passionately cherished programs generates bonds of lasting kinship and respect which cannot be forged as well as by pious exhortations from the pulpit to "love one another."

When a group of people unites in the furtherance of a greatly creative vision, whether the vision itself is the product of their community or the gift of one member to the rest, when men and women unite to create, they discover bases for interpersonal respect and loyalty far more persuasive than religious injunctions to be nice to one's neighbors. To proclaim the eternal significance of human creativity as an expression of God's will is to lay a firm foundation for truly loving community.

The third thing that happens when we fail to affirm the creativity of God in our sermons is that we almost inevitably exacerbate the problem of the miraculous in Scripture and tradition.

Whatever more the miracle may be, it is never less than testimony to the open-endedness of creation. It is at the very least the way in which human beings perceive the continuum from time to eternity, upon which no point is without the active presence of the divine love and the hope that it makes possible.

God's direct interventions in history, God's disruptions of what we regard as the normal flow of causality may on one occasion or another be prompted by divine justice or mercy. But the result is always to generate new possibilities where old ones have been exhausted. Whatever the actual mechanics of the Exodus, for example, it stands at the center of Israel's faith as powerful testimony to the power of a God who says, "Behold, I make all things new."

Commentators on religion have often noted the pathos of an American fundamentalism which, while insisting upon the literal historicity of all biblical miracles, generates by its overall approach to life a prosy vulgarity which rises like a mist from the swamp of blessed assurance and makes it exceedingly difficult for even the devout to catch a glimpse of the God who is active in history.

Whatever their position on the spectrum from conservative to liberal, many Christians by their almost exclusive emphasis upon God's redemptive act on Calvary accomplish the same unfortunate result. People for whom the miraculous is nothing more complex than a whimsical manifestation of occasional mercy will almost inevitably find it difficult to understand the miraculous as something relevant and available to them in any but the most legalistic sense.

When, however, our preaching speaks to that capacity for surprise and wonder that lurks somewhere in every human heart, when it directs attention away from that which is already settled and fore-closed toward that which is *open and yet to be*, it testifies as elo-quently as it can to that realm of infinite possibilities in which the miraculous is grounded. To know one's self as the instrumentality of an endless process, to understand one's self as being in some sense *history's open end*, is to view the miraculous in a new and more per-suasive perspective. Then the particular miracle becomes not an arbitrary compassionate or wrathful intrusion from beyond the boundary of time, but a possibility inherent in every moment.

Honest Christians have always differed about the mechanics by which the miraculous manifests itself in particular times and places. And they will probably always differ about this. But preaching which gives appropriate emphasis to divine creativity can provide the best basis for facing those differences honestly and dealing with them in a constructive fashion, because it not only validates but encourages those qualities of imagination, that sense of mystery without which such discussions become far too often dogmatic squabbling.

The fourth deficiency of preaching that neglects to proclaim God the Creator is that it allows, even encourages, men and women to excuse the expression of their own creative energies from the disci-pline of God's judgment. It encourages people to regard their vitali-ties as being only incidental to the will of God in life. And in so doing it tends to free life's energies from the restraints essential to their highest development.

Like the old monk whose words about celibacy I quoted earlier, many of us are inclined to rule all generative powers outside the juris-diction of proper Christian concern. And when we do this, whether with human sexuality, economic enterprise, or our aesthetic compo-nents, we create a kind of moral twilight zone in which we some-times feel at liberty to function in free-wheeling fashion, evaluating our behavior, if at all, in terms of subjective criteria which fail to fulfill one of the primary duties of moral sensibility, that is, to pro-vide standards for the direction of human behavior in community.

As I suggested earlier in passing, many self-consciously "pro-phetic" sermons against social irresponsibility, against exploitation of the weak, neglect of the poor, and so on, fall on deaf ears, not necessarily hard hearts. They deal with matters about which even genuinely committed men and women have learned to distrust the pulpit's realism, if not its fairness. Many of the churches' most impas-sioned and thoughtful declarations about social issues often seem totally irrelevant to the concerns of those for whom justice, as such, is not life's primary objective.

One of the most mutinously angry groups of Christians with which I have ever had to deal was the Social Action Committee of a small Methodist church which had just encountered for the first time the allegation that "God is on the side of the oppressed." The members of the committee were conscientious and for the most part politically liberal men and women. But they were outraged by what one of them called "this attempt to put God into uniform."

People can be honestly interested in building more humane communities and still recognize and value the inevitable tension between creativity and justice. And when they repeatedly hear sermons in which the tension is unimaginatively, facilely, and inevitably resolved in favor of the preacher's definition of justice, when God is declared to be present only at that end of the spectrum, they cannot help being turned off, even angered. They conclude that the social message of their faith has no real understanding of or applicability to their creative energies. So they turn those energies over to nonreligious standards of motivation, guidance, and review.

One of the horrors of the demonic power that we call Nazism was its effort to free the vitalities of the human race from what it regarded as the paralyzing inhibitions of Christian morality. Its attempt to resolve the tension between creativity and justice in favor of wholly amoral energies provides an extreme example of what can happen when traditional religion fails to speak relevantly to the creative impulses so inherent in truly human being.

I have come increasingly to feel that one of the infirmities of the *pulpit* version of the social gospel, as distinguished from the more thoughtful scholarly treatments of the subject, was its tendency to formulate one normative social creed, a creed which appeared to denigrate creativity as unimportant. One of the differences in point of view between the brothers Niebuhr, Reinhold and Richard, was the latter's serious doubts about the wisdom of the Christian Socialist movement. (Reinhold eventually came to share those misgivings.)

The fifth and final problem engendered for our preaching by the neglect of creativity is one with which I shall deal at more length in my next chapter.

As I have listened for forty years to students struggling to speak persuasively about God's redemptive zeal, I have come to believe that our ability to do that important job depends upon giving much more substance to the life in Christ than we have been able to give it in the past. One might put this epigrammatically and say that preachers are disposed to talk too much about what people are saved *from* and too little about what people are saved to.

At one time this problem was far less serious than it is today. People were saved from hell and to heaven. But these words do not have the compelling power which they once apparently packed, even though their substance is still to be reckoned with daily. And the semantic substitutes that we have used to replace them, particularly those which correlate with heaven, seem to lack impact. Preachers do a pretty fair job of convincing people that they want to avoid anxiety, estrangement, alienation, rigidity of personality, and similar states of personal wretchedness. These ills pervade the human condition, and no one has a good word for them.

When, however, we move to the positive side of the message we frequently falter badly. We have words and phrases with which to state the alternatives to what people want to be delivered from. But our words and phrases lack authority when they are not rooted in an appreciation of God's creativity as both gift and imperative. If the result of God's action in Jesus Christ is rebirth, new life, preachers need to find ways of talking about that life which make it more appealing than an eternal revival meeting or what Halford Luccock once called "an endless succession of rainy Sunday afternoons."

People *can* be helped to understand and to appreciate the spiritual value of their constructive energies. And only when they do can we preachers present salvation as something more than a bit of celestial bookkeeping or a stagnant sort of self-acceptance.

Let me close with a somewhat extended analogy that sums up what I have been saying.

When the Yale Divinity School was built, very few students and not all faculty members owned automobiles. Most of those who studied at the school or visited there approached along a thoroughfare called Prospect Street. Knowing that this would be the case, the architect who designed the quadrangle arranged its buildings in such a way that they could be appreciated from the avenue of general access. One enters the front gate and looks up a slight rise and over a splendid lawn toward the chapel, which is the visual and spiritual center of the school.

As more and more people began coming with their own automobiles, however, it became necessary to provide parking spaces in greater abundance than those available in the original back lot. So a large field to the north of the quadrangle was taken over and paved for that purpose.

Now most of those who study or visit the seminary enter by a small door opposite the new lot, a door that was originally intended as a delivery door. Hundreds of people have entered and left the complex over the years, always through that small entrance, over which, in an effort to dignify it, a kind of Georgian canopy was eventually built.

Then each spring when the graduating class marches to the foot of the campus, to the front gate to meet the faculty column and return in procession to the chapel for the baccalaureate service, some young man or woman looking back along the tree-lined vista will say in surprise and wonder, "Good Lord, I've never really seen this place before!"

It is, I suggest, one of the tasks of the preacher as theologian so to speak of the creating God that men and women who have entered the realm of faith, as all must, by the delivery door on Calvary will be led in time to Prospect Street, to see something of what the divine architect dreamed "in the beginning."

# CHAPTER 4

# Confronting
## God
### as Judge

There are in the New Testament passages which have come to be known as "the hard sayings of Jesus," verses in which the Nazarene is reported to have said or done things that do not square with the popular understanding of his personality and mission. These are incidents that tend to offend most modern readers.

One of the most troublesome of these hard sayings occurs in the fifteenth chapter of Matthew. It concerns an encounter between Jesus and a woman described simply as a Canaanite. The Master and his disciples, you will recall, are in the country around Tyre and Sidon, when a woman comes to them in great anguish. Her daughter is ill, possessed by a demon. And she cries to Jesus for help. Prompted by his followers to turn her away, Jesus says, "I was sent to the lost sheep of the house of Israel." And when she persists in pleading her cause he replies, "It is not fair to take the children's bread and throw it to the dogs."

This incident causes as much squirming in the pulpit as any section of the Bible. Here is the kind of human crisis that is almost always able to elicit the sympathy and help of decent people. A plea on behalf of a sick or endangered child will melt hard hearts and send even the slothful hurrying on errands of mercy. But the Nazarene rejects the woman's appeal and tells her that she is a dog who has no claim on his healing gifts.

There are various interpretations of this upon which even the pulpit relies from time to time. Occasionally it is alleged that Jesus was simply testing the woman's faith, making her crawl a little to prove her confidence in his power and that he intends from the first to

56

grant her request. Some preachers make of the story an effort on the part of the Master to teach his disciples a lesson in interethnic relations. They had, so such sermons go, been somewhat arrogant in dealing with the people around Tyre and Sidon, and Jesus wanted to show them how this kind of thing looked to others.

Then there are those who attribute the whole episode to Jesus' famous sense of humor, that last resort of preachers for dealing with difficult passages in the New Testament. This gambit begins, "Oh, how Jesus' eyes must have danced under his heavy black brows as he said this." And we are invited to imagine the disciples rolling on the ground, holding their sides in paroxysms of uncontrollable mirth, at this witty sally by the "man of sorrows and acquainted with grief" at the expense of the suffering mother of a sick child.

Well, it is a lot easier to poke fun at other people's interpretations of such passages than it is to make sense of them for one's self. But it seems to me with the passage of time and as I observe the mood of our own age, that we have so much trouble with *this* text because it says something significant about divine *judgment* that we simply do not want to hear. We will often go to absurd lengths hermeneutically to avoid facing the complexity of God's presence in history, to avoid confronting the hard reality of God's justice.

The meeting between Jesus and the Canaanite woman is far more than an encounter between two personalities. It is, I shall argue, symbolic in biblical terms of two radically opposed world views. And the implications of the incident go far beyond mere comment on the character of the man Jesus of Nazareth.

The Canaanite woman represented for the Jew a pagan view of the cosmos. For her no ultimate consistent purpose underlay human experience. There was not one God whose intending will shapes history, but a multiplicity of warring deities whose petty whims and antagonistic ambitions made a nightmare of creation. A sufficiently clever person could play the balance of power and manipulate these divine dilettantes to his or her advantage. And the appropriate function of religion was not to learn and do the will of the gods but to control or evade it.

Jews, as we know, regarded the cosmos as the province of one God whose single purposing will established order in creation and gave a degree of dependability to human existence. They were bowed under a sense of the righteousness of the Most High and the realization that even ritual purity was virtually impossible of attainment.

Jews understood all too well that acts have consequences and that sin would eventually bring down upon their heads the wrath of Heaven.

Now from what I have said earlier it should be clear that in my mind paganism and Judaism represent in a significant sense the extremes on a spectrum, both of which overstate aspects of the human experience of the divine. The pagan was realistic in realizing that one cannot plot exact and dependable ways of dealing with the mystery of existence, ways which will assure the functioning of a precise natural or moral causality. But the pagan was wrong, of course, in supposing that the insecurities of human experience in history reflect accurately the nature of ultimate reality, that there is, in fact, no single purposing will behind the paradoxes inherent in finitude.

The Jew, on the other hand, was right in insisting upon that ultimate unity which undergirds the cosmos, but wrong in believing that it can be fully known and so diligently obeyed as to assure the faithful of absolute security and successes.

It seems obvious to me that Jesus' meeting with the Canaanite woman presented him with a painful dilemma. Could he do for her daughter what she asked?

Unfortunately, the common homiletic interpretation of this passage casts that question in the jurisprudential mode. That is, Jesus is assumed to be asking whether he had God's *permission* to grant the woman's request, whether she is a member of the club, as it were, and entitled to its privileges. And pursuing this line some commentators make much of the fact that in Mark's account of the story Jesus raises the question of priorities as between Jews and gentiles, saying that the children of Israel must be fed first.

But it seems more likely to me that what Matthew's Gospel raises here is not the jurisdictional issue at all, but the issue of *possibility*. The question before the Master is not does this woman deserve the healing mercy of God, but can this woman appropriate the healing mercy of God? Or to put it in more general terms, is there any substance to the concept of divine compassion separated entirely from an understanding of divine judgment?

Let me suggest an analogy here that is built into the very body of the narrative in both Matthew and Mark. (I emphasize that I use it only as an analogy, although I must confess that I am tempted to see the hand of the Holy Spirit in the fact that so apt an analogy is provided for us in the text itself.)

Jesus said to the woman, "It is not fair to take the children's bread and throw it to the dogs." Those whose business it is to know such things tell us that dogs derive virtually no nourishment from the bread on which human beings feed. Their digestive systems are not constituted to use the cereal grains effectively. (You may have seen the television commercial in which a young woman is shown being criticized by her husband for buying a dog food which contains barley. As she reads the label on the package in response to his prompting, she says indignantly, "Barley? Why, that's cereal. Dogs shouldn't be fed cereal.")

To feed a dog bread may do it more harm than good. For a dog that is fed nothing will find food on its own. It will hunt, scavenge, beg from strangers, tip over garbage cans, and so on. But a dog that is fed on bread may curl up quietly on its master's hearth and die of starvation. The bread will fill its belly and still the pangs of hunger—without providing any of the significant nourishment needed for survival. It will not sustain the blood, bone, and tissue in the animal's body.

"It is not fair to take the children's bread and throw it to the dogs." It is not fair to the children. But neither is it fair to the *dogs*.

Again, I am not suggesting that Jesus was a biologist and intended to make his point in this fashion. But the fact remains that the image that he used tells us more than he probably intended about the dilemma in which he found himself. It is one thing to proclaim the boundless mercy of God to those who hunger for mercy. It may be quite another thing to proclaim that grace to those who are quite unprepared to appropriate it. The point is not that the gift is wasted or lavished upon the unworthy. The point is that one may do mortal injury to the person to whom it is irresponsibly given.

The problem raised by Jesus' meeting with the Canaanite woman has in one form or another plagued the Christian faith throughout its history. Some of the earliest church leaders insisted that people must become Jews, must be circumcised, before they could be counted as followers of Jesus Christ. They believed that the gospel was intended for the "lost sheep of the house of Israel," for those who bore in their flesh the mark of their commitment to the mighty God by whom all of life is created, ordered, and judged.

This is obviously a complex issue. Admittedly, there is danger in simplifying it. But there is more to be said for the circumcision party than most Christians have been willing to admit. It raised a question to which Christianity has never found an entirely satisfactory answer.

From birth to death Christians are steeped in assurances of divine mercy. From one end of the theological spectrum to the other, our faith speaks the language of undemanding grace and abundant compassion. Whether expressed in the traditional form, "Just as I am without one plea," or the more current jargon of a psychologized self-acceptance, personal fulfillment theology, the message tends to be the same. Heinrich Heine summed it up well in his infamous dictum, "I love to sin. God loves to forgive sin. Really, this world is admirably arranged."

Occasionally preachers remember that there is something in the Bible about judgment. They reach under the pulpit, take out masks of wrath, hold them up before their faces and intone from the diaphragm that "God is a righteous God who hates iniquity." And at this point the people in the pews who have learned how to play this liturgical game, if no other, delve into the hymn book racks, take out little masks of fear and contrition that have been provided for their use, hold them up before their faces and offer ritualistic acknowledgments of their most grievous faults.

But we all know that this is a kind of charade, don't we? That behind that preacher's mask of wrath is the familiar countenance of the endlessly smiling Jesus. And that in the last few minutes of the sermon the preacher is required by the rules of the game to set aside that angry face and scatter forgiveness with a lavish hand.

Now it would be easy to interpret what I have just been saying as the charge that people self-consciously and cynically presume upon the mercy of God, that they deliberately behave in irresponsible ways, relying upon Christ to make it all right in the end. And there is more validity to that charge than the ease with which we often dismiss it would suggest.

Paul foresaw the danger and asked, "Shall we continue in sin that grace may abound?" And while his Pharisaic background and deep-rootedness in the law prompted him to respond, "By *no* means!"— generations of Christians since, raised on endless assurances of unconditional mercy, not rooted deeply in the Law, have tended to cry, "By *all* means!"

Martin Luther had to deal sternly with German Protestants who indulged in flagrant immorality in order to demonstrate their reliance upon grace and grace alone. At one period in its history the

Church of Scotland found itself beset by witchcraft and satanism in which even local church leaders participated as a manifestation of their total confidence in divine compassion. Every age in the history of our religion has been afflicted by some version of what might be called an "indulgences psychology," the feeling that salvation can be appropriated and retained without reference to the quality of one's personal behavior.

Human beings *have* always been willing to presume in quite cynical ways upon grace, and still are. It is one of the less admirable aspects of recent liberal theologizing that it has tended to scoff at the notion, regarding it often as a mere remnant of the doctrine of total depravity from which the Enlightenment rescued the human race.

But the deliberate abuse of divine mercy is by no means the whole story, nor even the major part of it. The preoccupation of preaching with God's redemptive love has subtler and more corrosive consequences. It has tended in various ways to confuse people about the nature and limitations of love itself. And in so doing it has encouraged modes of behavior which are often seriously damaging to human personality. Men and women with no conscious inclination to "sin the more that grace may abound," people who honestly mean to relate in loving ways to the world around them, frequently fail to do so, because they do not understand what love means and implies for finite creatures.

Many years ago I was called upon to counsel a young couple whose marriage was in serious trouble. This does not happen to me very often. I am simply not the counseling type. (I can't stand all those long silences!) And the only reason that I had been called into this crisis was that I had been the best man at my friends' wedding, which apparently persuaded them that I had a vested interest in the success of the enterprise.

At one point when the young husband had just finished some blatantly self-serving statement about their problems, his wife burst in angrily, "But, Bob, you're being so unfair! You're always so unfair!"

Bob's response was to lean back in his chair, give his bride what can only be described as a hooded glance and say throatily, "When we were married I promised to love you, not be *fair* to you."

At this romantic gambit the foolish young woman fell into his arms and they were reconciled, just long enough to conceive a child. Then the marriage ended in divorce. And two years later Bob killed himself.

That tragedy has remained deeply imbedded in my mind, because for me it is symptomatic of the general human condition. Bob was not destroyed by some wrathful thunderbolt from heaven, occasioned by his marital irresponsibility. Bob destroyed himself by ignoring the structures of justice from which even love is not exempt. And in her own way his wife connived in his self-deception. Both were in part victims of a Christian ethos in which *love* is highly romanticized, regarded as an omnipotent force which liberates the individual from anything that suggests patterns of responsibility and bestows upon him or her an almost infallible, instinctive capacity to know what is right and good.

This tendency is most vividly visible, of course, in interpersonal terms. Parents sometimes dominate and distort the lives of their children by autocratic, even *cruel* behavior which they justify to themselves and when necessary to others on the basis of their parental affection for their offspring.

I sat one afternoon in a courtroom and saw a young woman being tried for child abuse. She had caught her five-year-old son taking pennies from her purse. And in order to teach him the evil of his ways she had held his hand over the gas flame on the kitchen stove. Unfortunately she held the hand too close to the flame for too long. And for the rest of his life that child will have one hand and one withered claw.

As she made her defense to the judge that day, the mother kept repeating, "I *love* my son. How could I do anything to cripple him. I *love* him too much for that."

In the face of the indisputable fact that she had hurt the boy grievously, she offered *love* not simply to justify but to deny the reality of what had happened.

In the relationship of the sexes the plea "After all, we love one another, don't we?" has been used to rationalize unnumbered unconsecrated and irresponsible couplings, couplings so common and careless that the multitude of purely optional abortions performed in its hospitals every year has become a heaviness in this nation's heart and a dangerous division in its spirit.

So blatant is this tendency among us that an avant-garde clergyman speaking to divinity students a few years ago declared that he regarded sexual fidelity as a repressive concept, one which prevents people from loving one another fully. And he expressed the hope that ministers might soon be liberated from this captivity, so that they could love all members of the congregation more freely.

Many of us who heard that talk were amused by what struck us as its patent absurdity. We are no longer amused. Time has overtaken that speaker. And his attitude seems almost square in contrast to those increasingly popular in society today. One college faculty member writing in a volume on human sexuality informed the reader that it will be necessary in the near future for Christians to change many of their sexual values, including their feeling about "bestiality," sex between human beings and animals.

Now I do not mean to suggest that such views are in any sense typical of Christian thought. But I am prepared to argue that they mark the boundaries of the absurd toward which some religious discussion is moving as it tries to define love apart from some of the traditional canons of responsibility and the hard reality of divine judgment that gives meaning and form to life in history. When one takes the most simplistic version of Reformation theology, reduces it to Paul Tillich's doctrine of *acceptance*, and proclaims the result in the vocabulary of a value-free psychology, the result can be a tragic corruption of the gospel—to the detriment rather than the cure of souls.

The effort to interpret divine mercy apart from divine judgment and its resulting vulgarization of love may threaten the integrity of human personality and relationships most visibly today in the area of sexual behavior. But it manifests itself in many other forms as well, among them the almost classic tendency of parents to substitute a kind of smothering love for justice in dealing with their children.

One can pursue this theme more helpfully, however, by crossing the artificial line which divides the interpersonal from the social and reflecting a bit upon what our irresponsible concept of love does to the communities of which we are all parts.

As is so often the case for people of my generation, Reinhold Niebuhr strikes the note on which we might begin. "I am never as dangerous," he said once, "as when I act in love. When I act in anger or aggression I put my conscience, my victim, and the community on guard. But when I act in love I disarm conscience, victim and community and am free to do my worst with neither let nor hindrance."

In an age in which theological students are inclined to think of

Reinhold Niebuhr as something that comes in no-return bottles I should like to require them to bind those words upon their hands, make them as frontlets between their eyes, and inscribe them upon the doorposts of their houses. "I am never as dangerous as when I act in love."

Just as human beings in their interpersonal relations are tempted to offer love as a cheap, convenient substitute for fairness, so in our social roles are we prompted often to the same distortions of the faith. This has been most obvious, of course, in the common tendency of Christians to propose love as the answer to complex economic and political problems for which more institutionally sophisticated solutions are required.

For unnumbered generations white Christians in this country exhorted blacks to eschew political action to improve their lives and urged them to rely on the good will and affection of their morally sensitive neighbors to do away with gross exploitation. Employers of labor, not too long ago or far away, resisted the formation of unions and explained that because they "loved" their workers, they could be counted upon to protect their interests better than "outside agitators." And women are still being advised in some quarters to abandon their struggle for legal protections and depend for their dignity upon the "love" of their fathers, brothers, husbands, and sons.

It is common to consider such arguments as sheer hypocrisy. And I am certain that many hypocrites have used them lavishly and cynically. But to a greater degree than many of us care to admit, such contentions arose from and reflected a quite honest misunderstanding of human experience, a misunderstanding rooted in significant part in the Christian denigration of divine judgment.

Men and women who have been taught by their preachers to see God fully disclosed in the compassionate Christ almost inevitably misunderstand and undervalue the institutional patterns within which community takes shape and the dynamics by which those patterns are related to one another. Social processes tend to be interpreted by them as merely the outward manifestations of all-important internal attitudes, susceptible to radical transformation by the mere amendment of those inner states of being.

The late Dean Liston Pope of Yale said on at least one occasion, "If every human being in the world were to accept Jesus Christ as personal Saviour, the world would probably not be much worse than it is now." And I also recall the angry comment of one of Dean Pope's younger colleagues in ethics who stormed out of the common room after a panel discussion of some political issue, muttering, "Sometimes I get sick and tired of this damned '*spiritual*' Christianity."

Neither of these men, I am sure, would have wanted to be permanently committed to all of the implications of those comments. Both were reacting, perhaps overreacting, to this very phenomenon. Their studies of societies and the people who make them up had persuaded them that history is more complex than the shadow of human character cast upon the earth: that social structures have, as it were, lives of their own which need to be taken seriously and understood by those who seek to build a more humane world. And they believed that it is not only wrong but dangerous to ignore this fact. Their conviction is well substantiated by the long record of indifference to social justice demonstrated by many devoutly religious people.

The literate members of mainline Christian churches in our time are likely to have a reasonably sophisticated awareness of their social responsibility, whatever the degree of their sacrificial commitment to discharge it. But there is a more subtle form of this problem that needs to be discussed in order to round out the topic of the importance of proclaiming divine judgment.

Back in the fifties the late Arthur Koestler, author and one-time communist, spoke about the efforts of the Soviet Union in its early, optimistic years to humanize criminal justice. Marxist theory, he pointed out, traces antisocial behavior to environmental factors. Crime is seen to be caused by oppressive social and economic conditions. When such conditions have been eliminated, the argument goes, crime will virtually disappear. But during the transition from an unjust to a just society, Lenin had taught, those who violate the law must be reformed and re-educated, not punished. Courts must recognize that the individual is not really to blame for his or her misdeeds and respond with compassion rather than retribution. The principle, said Koestler, was admirable and had much in common with the precepts of liberal religion. But before long it began to become clear that those whom we do not blame we do not regard as responsible. Those whom we do not regard as responsible we do not see as fully human. And those whom we do not see as fully human we are willing to twist and manipulate to suit our own convenience.

The way in which dissenters are treated in the Soviet Union today testifies to the prescience with which Koestler spoke. People who set themselves to any significant degree against the government are less and less frequently sent to prison or into exile and more and more often locked up in mental hospitals. They are not evil or really principled, goes the official line. They are simply sick, insane, more to be pitied than censured. By this device dissenters are removed from the community, and whatever they have said or written is dismissed as the ravings of a lunatic. What masquerades as social compassion is in reality an outrageous form of oppression.

Somewhat closer to home the United States has had a disenchanting experience with something called the "indeterminate sentence," that is, one in which the convicted criminal is confined not for a set period of time, but until he or she has been reformed and made ready to return to society. Some of the progressive penologists who were in the vanguard of those favoring this principle as essentially compassionate have now turned vehemently against it, because it has led to abuses worse than those it was intended to correct.

One can see this same reality demonstrated somewhat more subtly in other areas of modern life. There are today psychotherapists of solid reputation who urge us to stop treating alcoholics as "sick" people because this designation, originally intended to substitute compassion for moralistic indictment, has turned out to be for many alcoholics the perfect excuse to linger in the shadow land of their problem. More and more professional counselors are adopting the position taken by the columnist Ann Landers, who advised the long-suffering wife of one drinking husband to pack his overnight bag, put it on the front porch, make a reservation for him at the nearest Howard Johnson's and bolt all the doors to the house.

Parents today are hearing a great deal about something called "tough love," the need to stop endlessly "understanding" and start judging, so that wayward offspring have a chance to learn that there are forms to life, structures of responsibility which cannot be safely transgressed repeatedly. And there are minority group leaders who have begun to raise questions about some kinds of affirmative action programs which—compassionate purposes notwithstanding—can generate in the minds of children the ugly suspicion that they are inferior and cannot stand up to the competitive tests by which their peers are evaluated.

In an imperfect world where imperfect programs are administered by imperfect people, compassion can be a dangerous ground upon which to build social policy.

Now my purpose in speaking of these things is not to suggest that preachers should urge people to be less compassionate than they may feel inclined to be. It is my point, rather, that compassion separated from judgment is too often self-defeating. And that we need in our preaching to help Christians understand the appropriate relationship between the two. I do not propose a return to hellfire and damnation theology. Quite the contrary. I am persuaded that we cannot really free people from that jurisprudential nightmare unless and until we help them understand judgment in ways that square with what they know to be the realities of human experience.

You see, human beings understand that they are judged, even if they cannot or will not state their perceptions in theological terms. If you leap off the top of a ten-story building, you will hit the ground and go "Splat!" and die. And saying "Jesus, Jesus, Jesus" all the way down does not alter the result. If you treat other people in cruel and exploitive ways, they will come to hate you, and you will in time learn to hate yourself. And even going to church regularly and passing the "Peace" with fatuous bonhommie will not save you. A society which celebrates death, whether by the stockpiling of redundant weaponry or the *casual* use of abortion, will destroy itself. And no amount of ethical ratiocination will prevent that consequence. At some level people understand that. They know that they are judged, that there are finalities in life.

So when we preachers speak of divine mercy in ways that take no account of judgment, when for the traditional formulation that God is Creator, Judge, and Redeemer we substitute Creator, Redeemer, Sustainer, we omit from our definition of the divine that which is most inescapably *real* in human experience. And in so doing we lower tragically the level of our credibility with intelligent men and women. If preachers are as wrong about divine mercy as they are about divine judgment, people reason, then we are indeed lost. Our "Good News" becomes ironically a mere legalism when it is proclaimed in ways that give it no rootedness in the obvious facts of daily life. Those who are not vocationally committed to unraveling the tangled skein of Christian doctrine, men and women for whom religion is a resource, not a profession, can believe in God's mercy *only* when it is shown by their preachers to be in constant interaction with God's judgment. And the common habit of parroting the phrase "law and gospel," as though the mere repetition of the words explains something important, is a kind of clerical cop-out. Even

Martin Luther had trouble making sense of the relationship between law and gospel within the jurisprudential framework.

As long, therefore, as preaching fails to take judgment seriously and does not relate it quite explicitly to redemption in ways that make sense for the common daily life of the race, the ancient images of divine judgment as sheer retribution, as post-mortem pain, hellfire, and damnation will linger as a nasty suspicion in people's minds. In our well-meaning efforts to banish that concept of divine wrath we can actually reinforce its power. By refusing to bring the idea of judgment in persuasive ways into the rational discourses of faith and to give it a significant place in our proclamation of the gospel, we create a kind of pop dualism and turn primordial myths into fearful specters that haunt the fringes of piety with all of the ghost's power to inspire dread. When honest men and women look candidly at the turbulence of history in the light of preaching that has little or nothing to say about judgment, the most comforting conclusion they can draw is there is much truth to the old Russian legend that God has an idiot brother who is sometimes left in charge of the store!

It is, I believe, fair to say that masses of intelligent moderns, whatever their doctrine on the subject, dread hell in a gut-rending, mindshattering way that is as painful as anything that their greatgrandparents experienced—not in spite of our assurances of God's mercy, but because of them. Hell retains a psychological grip on people for whom it has no theological validity at all. And it will continue to do so, as long as Christian preaching fails to deal responsibly with the theological aspects of the subject.

On more than one occasion I heard Reinhold Niebuhr tell of a wealthy man whom he knew who set out one day to improve a public image that had been badly tarnished in his rise to wealth and power. He began to give liberally to various philanthropic foundations, agreed to serve on committees promoting one good cause or another, and started treating his employees in a somewhat more humane fashion than had been his custom. His motive in all this, Niebuhr would point out, was quite cynical. He wanted to improve his *image* in the public mind, *not* his way of life.

But then a strange thing happened. The man discovered to his own surprise that he enjoyed his new role in the community. It was pleasant to have people think well of him, and the civic work that he was doing gave him genuine satisfaction. The upshot of the whole process, Niebuhr concluded, was a profound, not a superficial transformation of the man's character.

Now clearly this experience was a manifestation of grace and the strange ways in which it moves in life. But it was grace mediated through judgment. Niebuhr's friend did not undergo some mysterious warming of the heart while reading the Bible. Nor was he stirred to love by a poignant encounter with some dramatic human need. Grace reached him through the judgment of God mediated by the disapproval of his neighbors. The indictment of his way of life by the community wrought changes more profound than any he contemplated.

Niebuhr's story also says something about the vexatious dichotomy between faith on the one hand and works on the other which theologians love so to moot, and which most lay people find at best confusing and at worst downright silly.

You see, when we preachers, in our zeal to offer hope to troubled congregations, leap too immediately and easily to what we have been taught to regard as everywhere and always good news, we may be guilty of frustrating rather than expediting what might be called the chemistry of salvation. The gospel can become as merely legalistic as anything promulgated by the Pharisees when it offers a word which, however positive it may be in principle, reacts negatively upon the metabolism of the sinner. One does not help the airsick traveller by repeated assurances that the plane is in no danger of crashing, if the sufferer's only hope is that the plane will crash as promptly as possible!

I suspect that lay men and women understand somewhat better than their spiritual mentors the real relationship between judgment and mercy. Because they, like their preachers, live with that relationship every day. But, unlike theologians, they have not learned to blur the hard reality and confuse the mind or insulate themselves against its real meaning by formulations of doctrine which must be repeated almost constantly in order to hide the truth.

When, for example, a husband who has strayed from the path of marital fidelity is reunited with his offended wife, he knows very well that he has not really been forgiven merely because the appropriate words of mercy have been spoken. Nor is he likely to be persuaded when his spouse sends him off to the office every morning with protestations of pardon and peace and receives him each evening with reminders that he has been forgiven, has his pipe and slippers and the newspaper neatly folded to the sports section by his favorite chair. Such "reassurances" are as damning as anything hurled at sinful Israel by Jeremiah. Our erring husband knows that he has been forgiven the day his wife tells him to get off his behind and dry the dishes.

You see, we can believe in forgiveness not when we are restored simply to the joys, amenities, and privileges of a ruptured relationship. But when we are restored also to the expectations, responsibilities, and burdens of that relationship. And even to some measure its exploitations and injustices.

James Martineau once wrote that those who are forgiven too often and too easily may lose the capacity to sin and sink to the level of *natural necessity* in their actions. There are, I am persuaded, a great many Christians in our churches today who live wretchedly at the level of natural necessity. Because they do not know what it means to be *judged*, they do not really understand the nature of sin. And because they do not really understand the nature of sin, they cannot truly know what it is to be forgiven. Oh, they can define redemption, perhaps, and sing hymns about the wideness of God's mercy and the profligate character of grace. But at the deeper levels of their consciousness, the message has no meaning at all.

Now I do not suggest that preachers need to teach people to sin. We do need, however, to speak of divine judgment in ways that give what might be called dignity to sin. For all our sophisticated reminders to the congregation that sin is a state of mind, the impulse to rebellion against God—not particular naughty actions—for all of these assurances, we inevitably trivialize sin and encourage lay men and women to do the same, when, in our unseemly haste to get to the "good news," we imply that God does not give a literal damn about what we do with our lives, that the eternal is so eager to be about the business of redemption that our corruption gets overlooked in the whole process.

I have said that lay men and women often reveal a realism about this matter of judgment and mercy that is lacking in their preachers. Even in those denominations that put the most emphasis upon unmerited grace the laity will sometimes make it clear in any candid discussion that it fears divine wrath far more than it trusts divine mercy, that to the degree that it achieves something resembling obedience, it does so out of an intuitive feeling, if nothing more rational, that it does not pay to get on the wrong side of the Most High.

This attitude was expressed bluntly by a Lutheran layman with whom I chatted after the morning service at a small church in Pennsylvania. He had been introduced to me as a pillar of the congregation and a man beloved throughout the community for the rich abundance of his works of charity and responsible citizenship. In the course of our conversation I asked him, "Why is it that you put yourself out so often to serve your neighbors, when you claim to believe that we are saved by grace alone? Is it out of sheer gratitude to God for the gift of unconditioned love?"

The man thought for a moment and then replied, "Well, I guess that's the official answer, sure. I am saved by grace alone. But," and here he made a great show of pretending to look around to see if the pastor was within earshot, then he went on in a whisper, "But I figure, why take a chance?"

I am not suggesting that most Christians do whatever good works they do out of fear that they will be struck down by a bolt of lightening, if they fail to do good works. I am suggesting that they are very often prompted in part by the conviction that God expects something of them—and in some mysterious way which they do not understand their lives will be better, if they make some honest effort to meet that expectation. No amount of passionate reiteration of the word of unmerited grace will shake that conviction, not because people want to live in fear of God, but because they need to believe that there is form and meaning in their daily lives. And they sense that meaning must be earned, that even God cannot give meaning as a gift.

The journal of a country doctor who practiced in rural America early in this century contains the following case history. He had been called in to treat a small boy who was suffering from some kind of undulant fever. The ravages of the disease were not so highly dramatic, but the recurring character of the symptoms was depressing the child. Just about the time when he thought he was on the way to full recovery, the malaise would return. His morale suffered greatly. So that even when the medical evidence showed that he was getting progressively better, that each attack was less serious than the one before, the patient was unable to believe it and languished in bed more and more of the time. His parents did all that they could for him. They devoted much time to playing his favorite games, reading stories, fixing his favorite foods, and being endlessly patient with his frequent tantrums.

Then one day when the physician came for his regular visit he found the boy up, dressed, and playing vigorously with a new toy. Delighted but surprised by this development, the physician said, "Son, you're looking mighty perky this morning. What brought about this change?" The child thought for a moment, then replied, "I sassed my Ma this morning, and she spanked me."

Here is a paradigm of the human condition. Our ability to believe deeply in the healing love of God often depends upon our fear of divine judgment. Or to put that another way, if we preach only Christ, we cannot really preach Christ at all!

# CHAPTER 5

# Hoping
## in God
### as Redeemer

During the terrible years in which Nazi tyranny crouched like a savage beast upon a prostrate Europe, millions of men and women were thrown into those pits of degradation, the concentration camps. As we know now, most of those who were sent there died or were murdered. But some survived the full duration of the Hitler regime. They lived through days of backbreaking labor and nights of terror. Family and friends were snatched from them and brutally slain before their eyes. They went without food, clothing, and medical care. They were infested with vermin, riddled with disease, and sometimes betrayed by those they had every reason to trust, sold for a crust of bread, a second cup of thin soup, or a pair of tattered shoes.

And they lived for one thing: the day when the tyrant would fall and his hideous system would go down with him to destruction. The day when God or fate or whatever they chose to call it would tire of the madness, and they would go free. This was the hope that kept them alive, the hope to which they clung with a ferocity which often came to match the cruelty of their captors.

Finally, the dream came true. The armies of East and West met over the corpse of the Third Reich. The guards abandoned their posts. The probing searchlights went out. The barbed wire was cut. The prisoners were set free—and scores of them committed suicide.

They had survived the terror, the hunger, and the cruelty. They had overcome vermin, disease, and betrayal, but there was one thing that they could not endure: the lost of a sense of *purpose*. When the goal on which all their hopes were fixed had been won, when the day to which they had so long looked forward had arrived, life became too great a burden to bear. Men and women who had survived the worst that human cruelty and heedless nature could inflict upon them sometimes collapsed psychologically before a relatively minor pain or disappointment.

Most of us are like those tragic victims of the Nazis in at least one respect. Our ability to cope with the hardships and frustrations of life is likely to be conditioned significantly by our sense of purpose. When we feel challenged by some cause that has meaning for us, when we feel that we are moving toward some objective to which our suffering is incidental, that suffering is bearable to a degree that it would not be if it seemed to reflect the blind and pointless working of chance.

This fact of life was brought home to me some years ago by an incident which profoundly influenced my way of looking at the Christian faith and upon which I have had occasion to reflect often since its occurrence.

I was at a cocktail party when I was approached by a friend who had drunk more than he could handle. He stood swaying before me, glass in hand, and I could tell from the expression of preternatural solemnity on his face that he was about to pose one of those "deep questions" which the conjunction of alcohol and a seminary professor seems to engender in people.

"Muehl," he asked, "if I believed all your Christianity crap, do you know what I'd do?"

I have learned from experience that such questions are not meant to be answered. So I waited for him to continue, which he promptly did.

"As soon as my kids were born," he said, "I'd have them baptized, and then I'd cut their throats from ear to ear. So they'd go straight to heaven. Now you tell me, Muehl, why any man who loves his children should let them go through the heartaches of this life and run the risk of hell, if he can send them directly to heaven by a single thrust of the knife?"

Ordinarily I *resent* cocktail party protocol which forbids the discussion of anything more serious than a vasectomy. But in this instance I was grateful to our hostess who intervened to make us mingle. My friend's truculent challenge bothered me more than I would have admitted to him, and it still does. Why should anyone who loves his or her children let them go through the heartaches of life?

That encounter was for me what might be called a "revelatory experience." That is, it brought into sharp focus a concern that had been for some time haunting the fringes of my peripheral vision. My friend obviously believed that the emphasis of Christian preaching upon God's *saving* act in Jesus Christ erodes the purpose of human life and makes a pious charade of history.

Now the natural and perfectly proper response of the professional Christian apologist is to insist that the charge is based upon a false notion of what happened on Calvary, that the advent of God in Jesus Christ enhances rather than diminishes the significance of human life. But here, again, we see one of the points, perhaps the most important point, at which academic theology needs thoughtful interpretation by the pulpit if it is to be rightly understood by men and women who are not paid and set aside to think theologically. While experts in doctrine may be able to demonstrate the folly of my friend's anxiety to the satisfaction of other *experts* in doctrine, there is substantial evidence to suggest that their explanations are not even comprehensible, much less persuasive, to the laity.

In various more and less subtle ways a great many people in our time demonstrate serious doubts about the significance of life in Christian terms. In some this manifests itself in an outright hostility to all religion. In others it takes the form of a pervasive anomie, a listlessness about life in general and its spiritual dimension in particular. Many are driven, as I suggested in my third chapter, to a form of dualism in which they profess piety but allow their lives to be informed and evaluated by one secular dynamic or another. (These are the people who are all too easily and often dismissed simply as hypocrites.) All three of these groups share my intoxicated friend's suspicion that Christian emphasis upon God's *redeeming* love renders the struggles and painful decisions of life meaningless.

The fact that such suspicions are based upon gross oversimplifications of Christian theology does not make them any the less demoralizing for the individuals who entertain them or for the culture to which we belong. And if we are honest with ourselves, we shall have to admit, I am convinced, that in important respects those oversimplifications are happily tolerated, if not actively encouraged, by preachers who shun the burdensome responsibility to do more than pass on the chapter headings of their theological educations. It is not easy to talk intelligently about purpose in human life in the context of the christocentric hymns, liturgies, and appointed lessons that surround us. And it is even more difficult when the gospel is filtered through the radical grace formulations of the continental Reformation.

But the basic problem is as old as the faith itself. It surely underlay Paul's anguished cry, "Shall we continue in sin that grace may abound? God forbid!" It vexed Clement, caused trouble for Origen, and prompted the apostate emperor, Julian, to forbid Christians to teach in the imperial schools "because," he explained, "they do not believe in life. And no one who does not believe in life should be permitted to teach the young."

Martin Luther, in one of his better-known sermons, exhorted his congregation in these words, "So if you have any talent, any special gift, discard it, so that you may rely on the sweetness of grace alone." More recently such men as Teilhard de Chardin and Hans Kung have voiced concern about what they regard as the "dehumanizing" dangers in Christian doctrine, dangers summed up well by Nicholas Berdyaev when he wrote, "The assurance of unmerited grace is undoubtedly a great consolation. But it carries with it the danger of making human life seem flat, shallow and commonplace." And Billy Sunday is said to have declared on more than one occasion that the best fate that could befall anyone would be to accept Jesus Christ as Savior, walk out of the tent, and be hit by a truck and killed instantly.

So we come full circle back to my intoxicated friend, his children and the redeeming knife, and the question. Is the acceptance of Jesus Christ really "rebirth"? Or is it, in fact, a slow death? To put it another way, once you've risen from the dead, what can you do for an encore?

Now it is important to enter a caveat here. I am not under the impression that millions of men and women listen so attentively to simplistic interpretations of the gospel that they are persuaded to draw their plausible, if inaccurate, conclusions about life from what they have heard. The impact of religion in general and the gospel in particular upon individuals is always to a significant degree achieved through *cultural osmosis*. That is, men and women are exposed, willy nilly, to attitudes and values in the society around them, a great many of which reflect the religious commitments of other people, world views which they would disown if put to them as explicitly theological claims upon their own minds. So it is not only fair but necessary to look to a sample somewhat larger than that available in churchgoers to examine the impact of the gospel upon human personality.

Let me invite your attention, then, to the way in which certain life-denying tendencies in Christian thought are reflected in the popular culture of our time. Those who view a lot of cinematic and television drama, and here I speak from experience if not authority, have noted that in many of the plot lines developed by those two media the person who carries forward the action of the story, the protagonist, is a man or woman of *dubious* or downright *evil* reputation. And conversely when someone appears upon the scene who is clearly identified as "religious" he or she is very frequently depicted as some sort of "wimp," a nonentity whom no one could possibly respect or depend upon. (I can still hear the contempt in the voice of a typical John Wayne character when he confronted someone with the words "Wal, Preacher.") The most that could be expected of such a one was that he or she get out of the way and let the courageous and competent immoralist get on with the job.

The famous drama critic George Nathan wrote in the early part of the century that he was getting sick of plays which featured noble prostitutes and lovable thieves in heroic roles. Well, Nathan's criticism did not put an end to this popular dramatic device. We continue to be afflicted by hordes of whores whose hearts of gold constitute a veritable cardiac Fort Knox and alcoholic gunmen who in the nick of time turn their weapons to some socially constructive purpose, even while they are sneering at the very idea of social responsibility.

One who watches enough television will be tempted to conclude that the American frontier was subdued by dance hall hostesses and cold-blooded killers who, for eccentric reasons of their own, enlisted briefly and under articulate protest in the westward march of civilization.

Then there is, of course, the contemporary, urbanized version of the myth, of which Mickey Spillane's "Mike Hammer" is currently the most visible exemplar. Hammer is a dissolute, womanizing, heavy-drinking, and violent man who shoots first and asks questions later, if, indeed, he bothers asking them at all. But true to this fictional genre, he manages to serve the ends of true justice better than those plodding idiots into whose incompetent hands society has foolishly entrusted the job.

Now just in case those knights errant do not make the message clear enough, the public has more recently been gifted with J. R. Ewing and Alexis Colby of "Dallas" and "Dynasty" fame. Here are two thoroughly rotten people who lie, cheat, steal, and even conspire to murder. And the American viewing public has been taught to love them. Their fan mail is mountainous and includes many offers of marriage or a reasonable facsimile. And their faces sell almost anything when used in commercials.

This phenomenon has so intrigued students of society that several pollsters have done surveys in an effort to discover *why* such degenerate individuals are so popular with presumably decent viewers. The findings of those with which I am familiar can be summed up in this way: people see in these characters an elemental vitality, a full humanity which they fear is lacking in themselves. In the words of one fan, "J. R.'s a real man. He knows what he wants and goes after it."

To put the case in terms with which we are likely to feel more familiar, a great many men and women today see sin as the animating force behind vitality, courage, and imagination. Prostitutes, gunfighters and their urban counterparts, and the swinging villains of "Dallas" and "Dynasty" are posited over against conventionally "moral" personalities who have been in some way dehumanized by the prevailing value systems of the West. And people who, for various reasons, are unwilling to launch frontal attacks upon what they take to be the Christian denigration of life express their resentment by applauding those who are willing to do so. The delighted laughter with which even the clumsiest put-down of the clergy on stage or screen is greeted by the audience should not be interpreted in purely ad hominem terms, I am persuaded. Masses of human beings do see Christian rebirth as just a premature form of death.

At one of our faculty luncheons last year a group of us from various disciplines were discussing plays that we had lately seen at local theaters. In the course of that conversation we began to wonder why modern drama gives us so few truly heroic characters, why it seems to specialize in protagonists who are at best ambivalent about even basic decency. In the light of my own concerns about this, it interested me greatly that it was a New Testament scholar who suggested and defended the thesis that the ethos of the New Testament which so informs our world view is not conducive to heroism.

But we need not take our cues from the popular culture in this matter. Evidence of the same attitude in slightly different form can be found within the patterns of religion itself. Those who have studied the great revival crusades, for example, describe what one of them has called "conversion freaks," people who seem to make an avocation of being saved.

Wherever some charismatic evangelist sets up a tent or rents a hall the streets outside are sure to be lined night after night with battered school buses bearing the names of various sectarian groups from all over the country. And each evening when the altar call is given, members of these pilgrim delegations crowd the aisles as they make their way joyfully to the mourners' bench. And, it has been noted, sometimes the same people go forward several times in the course of a single week.

It is possible, I suppose, that those who engage in such repetitious behavior are egregious sinners who manage to fall from grace every twenty-four hours and need the help of the evangelist to make it through the night. But that, I suspect, is far too simple an explanation. They are, rather, I believe, personifications of the problem of which I have been speaking. They are people for whom the process is the promise. Being saved is the one dynamic that they have learned to see in religion. God has been presented to them so exclusively and dramatically in redemptive terms that they cannot imagine how to relate to the divine in any appropriate fashion beyond the experience of conversion.

So they linger forever on the borderline between condemnation and grace, because for them that is where the action is, that is the only place in which they can hope to encounter God. Like the man and woman who enjoy fighting because making up is so much fun, such people are sometimes calculatingly indifferent to the moral quality of their lives because being forgiven is the one spiritual experience open to them.

Oh, they may hand out tracts on street corners and moistly exhort their friends and neighbors to give their lives to Christ. Or they may become religious voyeurs, attending revivals to watch other people in the throes of repentance. But these things are all manifestations of the same low church liturgy. The whole focus of their piety is upon grace and the initiative of God alone. (And then some of us profess to be surprised when a number of these burning hearts are found capering around a *burning cross* some night!)

Now it is tempting in such a setting as this to dismiss the whole phenomenon as a manifestation of religious primitivism. The churches which most of us serve or attend rarely have revivals and produce few "conversion freaks." We can cluck our tongues and feel sorry for the simple souls who indulge in such ritualistic behavior, but that would be a mistake. For as we move toward the center of the denominational spectrum, away from sectarian piety, we encounter something of the same fundamental attitude in a slightly different form.

I remember, for example, attending a conference one weekend at a small college in the Midwest. A group of theologians and their hangers-on had been convened by some religious committee to discuss "Christian Relevance in a Suffering World." While the actual program was limited to the professionals present, a few local students had been allowed to sit in as observers. And at the end of the final session one of them was invited to comment on what he had heard. He did so in this somewhat plaintive way: "I've heard a lot of talk," he said, "about how eager God is to forgive us, no matter how badly we sin. But I've heard nothing about how God might be at work in our lives helping us to live the way we should. I almost get the feeling that the Christian has a kind of obligation to sin, so that God gets to do his thing."

Now lest you think that this young man was stupid or had not paid very close attention to the discussion, let me report that during one of those sessions, when I suggested the possibility that Christian emphasis upon redemption might tend to rob human life of its purpose, one of the other panelists, a man noted for his gift in interpreting theology to lay people, interrupted to say, "But don't you see? That's the very genius of the gospel. It tells us that life doesn't need a purpose. It's a gift!" And, again, lest you think that this statement represented simply some eccentric individual's outré theology, let me remind you of Ernst Troeltsch's statement that "It is the glory of the gospel that it reduces all earthly distinctions to insignificance."

Imagine yourself sitting in a pew somewhere after a week spent in struggling with difficult decisions, a week of painful efforts to do the *somewhat better* rather than the *much worse* and hearing "good news" of that kind. It was, I suspect, such an interpretation of the gospel which led a distinguished Christian layman, a man who has given much to both his denomination and various national and international councils of the churches, to say to me, "You know, Muehl, I realize that the decisions that I make at my desk every day have ethical implications. And I frequently ask ministers for advice. But they rarely have anything helpful to say. I have almost concluded that they would rather wait until I make a mistake and then assure me of God's forgiveness."

I realize that what I have been saying so far assumes what might be called in general terms a "conservative" theology, that is, a doctrine of the atonement in which the cross of Jesus Christ is seen as the central saving factor in the drama of redemption, a theology which tends to stress salvation from a sinful world rather than the transformation of life in history. The relationship between that Christology and the problem of purpose in human life is, I believe, something to which preachers need to give serious attention.

But what about liberal theology? Does the preacher get around the challenge by rejecting doctrines of blood atonement and proclaiming Jesus-the-good-example, God's image of perfect humanity, what one famous divine called "God's kind of guy"? Unfortunately not. Liberalism in its own way tends toward another version of the same dilemma, a paralyzing confusion about the substance and dynamic of the life of Christ.

Like conservatism which concentrates upon getting people through this world with minimal damage to their souls, liberal piety tends to stress another kind of redemption as the ethos of the human encounter with God. It is redemption within history, to be sure, but it remains overwhelmingly preoccupied with divine compassion. For the liberal, as for the conservative, God is experienced primarily, if not exclusively, at the juncture of condemnation and grace.

The threat from which humanity is to be saved in liberal doctrine is not so much the wiles of the devil or the snares of the world per se. It is human carelessness, ignorance, and cruelty. And the reward for a faithful response is a better world for future generations. But the modus operandi remains what it was in the conservative tradition: mercy, God's mercy, inspiring the mercy of a human being to save the world from its sinful, self-destructive follies.

Now as preferable as this may be to a view which defines all historical experience, except conversion, into insignificance, it still fails to provide men and women with a persuasive reason for being in the first place. On "the bottom line," as the current jargon puts it, liberal theology is as hung up on redemption as its conservative counterpart. And for that reason it shares the latter's difficulties in fleshing out the substance of new being.

For most liberal preachers the nature of God and of God's will for humanity are revealed fully in the life and death of Jesus of Nazareth.

Everything of consequence that needs to be known about the divine can be learned from the words and deeds of the Master. To be faithful to God is to take Jesus as the model for one's own life and ask in all things, with Bishop Sheldon, what Jesus would have done under similar circumstances. For the liberal preacher to be "in Christ" is to be "like Jesus," to be guided by a complex of maxims inferable from the New Testament.

Professional theologians would want to quarrel with my brief summary of liberal doctrine. They would very probably and properly insist that the whole thing is more complicated than I seem to have made it and that when rightly interpreted Christian liberalism need not strike at the nerve of human motivation.

But I am not so concerned about the condition of professional theologians. My concern is prompted by the kind of gospel that I have heard *preached*, both in my classes and in local churches for the past half century. The great majority of these sermons fall victim to what I have come to think of as "the fatal final third." That is, when they reach the point at which background and analysis must give way to some persuasive proposal for the enriching of faith and witness, far too many of them trail off into vague proposals that the listeners take up their crosses and try a little harder to be like Jesus.

Admittedly this theological position has produced a rich treasure of dedicated humanitarianism, people committed to causes that have made life on this earth far more tolerable than it might otherwise have been. Western civilization is deeply in debt to the liberal concept of discipleship, and it would be grossly ungrateful to ignore that fact in this discussion. But those for whom the simplistic imitatio Christi constitutes an adequate faith are, I believe, greatly outnumbered by the men and women for whom the image of Jesus as perfect humanity produces painful frustration and even the crippling of personality.

I was raised in a vaguely liberal Christian piety. It did little that I can remember to influence me explicitly in my childhood. But when I went off to college it was the ground upon which I stood in trying to understand the new world that was opening out before me. Under the influence of people such as A. J. Muste, Kirby Page, Muriel Lester, and Norman Thomas I tried to adopt a lifestyle of radical obedience to the God made manifest in Jesus Christ.

For me this meant taking Jesus as my model of human perfection and asking in life's decisive moments what he would have done under the same circumstances. I agreed with my pacifist friends that I could not imagine the Master sticking a bayonet into anyone's belly. But neither could I imagine him spending time and money accumulating luxury items for himself while there were people in the world going without the basic necessities of life. I felt powerfully drawn to an ascetic emulation of what I took to be the Nazarene's mode of being in the world.

Now I must confess that this radical discipleship was made somewhat easier for me because I was going through college on a shoestring budget. It would not be unfair to suggest that I was making a principle of a poverty which would in any case have been my fate. If I had joined the Franciscan order it would have meant a substantial increase in my standard of living.

But whatever the complex influences at work to encourage it, I was pretty deeply committed to a life of self-sacrifice, a life which ruled out even the most common luxuries enjoyed by those around me.

With the passage of time, however, and exposure to Christian thinkers somewhat more sophisticated than those brought to Ann Arbor by the Fellowship of Reconciliation, a disturbing realization began to dawn on me. The road on which I had set a tentative foot, I discovered, would lead not only to poverty of the most *material* kind but to a poverty of *personality* as well. I would not, I saw, ever be able to buy a hi-fi set or the records to play on it. And my days would be without the joy and inspiration of great music. I would not feel free to attend special lectures, buy books beyond those needed for my courses, take field trips that were optional forms of enrichment in various subjects, or join my less dedicated friends for an evening at the theater. My conception of the faith would have meant no trips abroad to see for myself the diversity of human communities, no summers spent in recreation at the shore or in the mountains with the refreshment of the soul that these things can provide. I faced a barracks existence unleavened by anything that might take bread from the mouth of one starving child anywhere in the world.

At this point I discovered Reinhold Niebuhr and began to see the infirmity in my doctrine of human nature. Mortal creatures, I realized, do not exist as purely spiritual beings in some kind of social vacuum. We are inescapably tied to both our physical necessities and to those material goods that are essential to the dignity of life among other people. A life of total self-sacrifice, I came to fear, could lead to the stunting of my personality and the eventual disintegration of the self altogether. For one determined to live *in* the world rather than withdraw into contemplation, commitment to sacrificial poverty was a very risky business. In short, without at that point ever having heard of Teilhard de Chardin, I received the truth in the previously quoted statement that every truly creative life demands its luxuries as well as its victims.

While I was still wrestling with the problem posed by my new self-awareness, I had as close to a religious experience as an Episcopalian is allowed to come. It happened at a concert by the university symphony orchestra for which no admission charge was made. On the program was a composition by Ottorino Respighi called "The Pines of Rome."

According to the composer's program notes, the piece represents the mood created in him by the various clusters of pine trees that occur in the Eternal City. The first movement depicts the Villa Borghese, a public park in which children romp around playing and calling out to one another. The second movement is meant to convey something of the atmosphere of the pines adjacent to the catacombs. And an eerie chant constitutes the main theme, as Respighi tries to portray musically the places in which early Christians gathered to worship. The third part conjures up visions of the Janiculum, a beautiful parklike hill where the nightingale sings in the moonlight.

But the closing movement is what touched me in a special way. It is called "The Pines of the Appian Way." It begins with the atmosphere of early morning as woodwinds and flutes evoke the image of farmers leading donkeys loaded with produce toward the city markets in Rome. There is a lazy and tranquil quality to the harmonies then. But very gradually the listener becomes conscious of a heavy rhythmic beat in the distance. Inexorably this sound drowns out all others, until it strikes like a sledge hammer on the ears of the audience. Then, the composer tells us, as the drumming sound reaches its crescendo, there bursts through the morning mist a Roman legion, its banners borne proudly aloft, its ranks straight and formidable, the sun glinting on its armor, its weapons clashing with every step, a Roman legion returning from some remote outpost of empire and making its way in triumph to the Capitoline Hill.

Well, I am told that it is not great music. But it is scored for double augmented brass, and when you have as much German blood in you as I do, doubled augmented brass is a kind of revelation.

As I listened to this composition, great or not so great, I came to see that the Roman Empire was one of the complex and majestic achievements of the human race, that with all of its flaws and even demonic perversions of its energies, it revealed something about the nature of God and the divine will in history that cannot be learned and obeyed by the study and emulation of one short life lived in a remote corner of the Mediterranean world. I found that I could not make God a prisoner of the incarnation, that some of my rebellion against the image of Jesus as human perfection was prompted by a selfish desire for comfort and security in life. But I also found that a large part of it, an important part, was also deeply rooted in a personal conviction about the significance of human history, which is, after all, one of the primary implications of God's self-disclosure on the cross.

Then I began to realize that when the people to whom I had been preaching for five years sadly dismissed my sermons while praising me for my piety, they were motivated not only by an ordinary human selfishness but by their own firmly planted belief that something of eternal significance about the will of God is revealed, as it were, in Rome. They could not forthrightly reject my message without casting away what they had always heard proclaimed as the gospel, Jesus the perfect person. But they could not accept my message without casting away many of the things that they knew were vital to their own human being.

You see, Jesus was possessed by the mercy of God. He came among us to proclaim God's redemptive love. And this fact determined both the content of his teaching and his mode of being in the world. He was sent to a people bowed for centuries under an intolerable burden of judgment, a people from whom absolute obedience to an absolute righteousness was demanded, a people for whom in the very nature of things such obedience was impossible. Jesus came to proclaim deliverance from that awful captivity. His mission dictated the substance of his message and the whole tone of his relationships with others. It is this fact that makes it impossible for anyone who is not courting martyrdom to imitate him. And this is to say nothing of the great range of special gifts and powers which tradition attributes to his divinity. What need has he of job security who can multiply loaves and fishes? Why need one fear death who has himself raised the dead?

You see, divine mercy is essentially *irresponsible* within history. Like creativity it cuts across the patterns of justice. It sweeps with anarchic freedom over the landscapes of this world, making possible the reconciliation of ancient antipathies and the salvation of even the most depraved. Divine mercy cancels the past and opens before us a future of infinite possibilities. Its real gift is neither rationalization nor excuse. Its purpose is not to explain why we have sinned and make us feel somewhat better about our corruption. Divine compassion offers not consolation but rebirth.

As the one in whom this love of God was incarnate, Jesus of Nazareth was compelled by his commission to live across the grain of these prudential counsels by which human existence in history is made possible. He walked the second mile, turned the other cheek to the smiter, forgave seventy times seven, and exhorted his followers to do the same. When people tried to get him to speak of justice or prudence he was more likely to respond with some radical counsel which mocked both justice and prudence. He walked knowingly into danger and rebuked those who loved him when they urged him not to go.

There are many reasons for the *elusiveness* of the historical Jesus. Not the least of these, I am confident, is the manner in which, while living within history, he set himself at so many points over against history, against the causal sequences of which it is inescapably composed. We have trouble finding him, because he defied and rejected those trajectories which enable us to predict where another might come down.

So Jesus' crucifixion was not the anomalous interruption of a well-balanced, perfect human life, a career from which all people might construct models for their own lives. His crucifixion was the inevitable and quite logical end of a life which challenged and in so doing denigrated many of the most basic human values. The true offensiveness of his message lay not in an attack upon the world's corruption, but in its attack upon those legitimate, even majestic, concerns which are essential to responsible existence in this world. What troubles so many decent men and women to this day is not what the gospel seems to say about their worst, but its obvious indifference to their hard-won and painfully defended best.

Now it has been suggested by some theologians that while the image of Jesus as perfect humanity is impossible of successful emulation, it is an ideal toward which men and women can strive, even though they realize that the goal can never be achieved. Having this model life before them, it is argued, will motivate believers to come as close to its quality as possible.

The primary failure of this Jesus-the-perfect-human-being ethic is its failure to take account of the propensity of normal people to be frustrated painfully when any standard is defined as quite beyond their reach.

I had an opportunity to see dramatic illustrations of this fact of life in the psychology laboratories at the University of Michigan when I was a student there. A team of psychologists was studying the mechanism of what was then called "the nervous breakdown." It had set up an experiment with rats in which the animal was forced by a stream of compressed air to jump from a platform toward one of two doors, each of which was marked by a special symbol. If the rat hit the right door, it found itself in the presence of food, drink, and another complaisant rat of the opposite gender. If it hit the wrong door, it banged its nose and fell into a charged net from which it received a mild shock.

After a while the rats learned to select the right door, the one that led to rewards. And then the symbols were reversed. Where they had learned to expect gratification they received instead punishment. Again they learned to adapt to the arrangement. And when they did the symbols were changed again. And so on for weeks.

The end result of these repeated frustrations was *not* ever-increasing zeal, greater efforts to choose correctly. Eventually the rats gave up entirely and when forced to jump one time too many went into a kind of catatonic trance, their limbs rigid and their eyes open but unseeing. Nothing could move them further at this point.

There are in our world, I am persuaded, far too many catatonic Christians, men and women whose paralysis of the spirit reflects not a lack of commitment but a perfectly natural human despair in the face of an urgent but admittedly impossible demand.

Here we can see more clearly than at any other point in this book, perhaps, the distinction between what I have called "academic theology" on the one hand and "homiletic theology" on the other. The image of Jesus as relevant but unattainable ideal can be a useful focus for discourse among professional Christian scholars who are about the business of opening up rather than answering questions. It suggests interesting avenues of speculation about the limits of human nature and challenges in ways that are more fructifying than frustrating. What academics receive from their ruminations on this subject differs markedly from what lay men and women hope to get from theirs.

For the people in the pews, theological discussion is not an entertaining end in itself. It is, rather, the means to an end. That end is greater clarity about the nature and will of God and a more substantial motivation for obeying it. Their religion is of necessity shot through with prudential concerns which give them little patience with impossible perfection, whatever the theoretical relevance of that perfection. And I have found that they deeply, if inarticulately, resent having what seem increasingly to them mere academic games foisted off on them from the pulpit as models suitable for emulation in their daily lives.

And, of course, this resentment is made all the more intense because at some level of the mind most people have entertained serious doubts about the claim that Jesus of Nazareth is in fact a perfect human being. The problem, you see, is not some simple gap between belief and action, but a serious doubt about the basic premise upon which this kind of theology is built. The Nazarene's obvious lack of interest in the data of their daily lives reflects less upon the *value* of those data than upon the *relevance* of the Jesus model.

Let me summarize the point in this way: the mercy of God made manifest in Christ does not enable us to live with a sublime indifference to the tensions of which history is composed. The mercy of God made manifest in Christ empowers us to take those tensions with dread-filled seriousness, confident that what they inevitably wound mercy will heal.

Jesus did not die gracefully to demonstrate the insignificance of life. He was slain for our sakes that we may have life and have it more abundantly. The more we exalt the Jesus model and declare that it suggests the possibility of perfection within history, the more doubt we cast upon the need for the divine and redeeming Christ.

This problem is a dramatic challenge for homiletic theologians because they are the ones who are charged to speak most immediately to the particularities of human experience and Christian witness. And it is only in the turbulence and challenge of those particularities and the daily summons to witness that the gospel becomes more than a vaguely religious idea. Thus, the best Christian preaching is always in some respects dated, because it takes with such profound seriousness the context in which it is preached that it may very well seem irrelevant or even foolish to those who come after us. The best preachers are expendable because they often lose the transcendent perspective completely in their effort to address the creature who dwells in time rather than eternity.

This is a difficult fate to accept. But the preacher must accept it if he or she is to meet the first demand of an effective homiletic theology, that it treat individual human lives with profound seriousness, not as mere illustrations for the important business of theology.

There are two elements in the proclamation of God's redeeming love which are most important. First, we need to set aside the pre-Copernican concept of human nature which informs so much of our traditional preaching. Henry James and Carl Lange have something to tell us on this score that needs to condition our interpretations of Paul, Augustine, and Luther. The flow of influence between what people believe and what they do is not a one-way street. Attitude and action interact more intimately and significantly than traditional piety is prepared to admit. The old man referred to in the fourth chapter set out one day to change his public image for quite cynical reasons, but the *actions* involved in doing so profoundly altered his whole view of himself and his life.

This is a reality of which we take too little account in our preaching, especially since Paul Tillich announced "acceptance" as the twentieth-century version of indulgences. Dorothy Soelle has criticized Christian neglect of a theology of *work* . Indeed, our deadly fear that people might try to earn their way into heaven has led us to overlook and badly underemphasize the impact of the job on the human spirit. We insist upon telling our congregations that in the last analysis eight hours or so of every day have little or no eternal significance, lest they begin to think too highly of works.

I am grateful to my colleague, Paul Holmer, who said musingly one day at coffee hour, "There are people in this world who seem haunted by the fear that God might some day in a fit of absent-mindedness allow someone to sneak into heaven on the basis of virtue rather than grace."

Too many such people inhabit our pulpits and pander to the notion that Christian faith is a vaporous thing that can be sprayed on any lifestyle and make it "O.K." And in so doing they mock the idea that there is content to the life in Christ, that what men and women do is not simply an expression or manifestation of their faith, but an important keystone in its structure.

While I was preparing this chapter I saw a television drama in which two people were discussing a third who was not present. "But," one of them said, "she's a prostitute!" To which the other replied, "Prostitute is what she does, not what she is."

Ponder the implications of that distinction for a moment. "Prostitute is what she does, not what she is." That corrosive falsehood is in large part the pathetic gift of a quite outmoded concept of human nature, a concept in which a kind of Christian influence can be discerned. Being and doing flow back and forth in ways that make nonsense of the effort to separate them. And this raises serious questions about our theological commitment to the same kind of distinction between faith and works.

In looking for ways of thinking about this matter and speaking to it helpfully in our sermons it seems to me that perhaps we need to differentiate between the past and present tenses. That is, the works that have been done are a cancelled check and have no saving power at all. No one is justified in the sight of God by pointing to what occurred yesterday. But the possibilities in tomorrow, the options yet to be exercised, the work to which we may turn our hands and minds in the future—these things, I would argue, are inescapably important ingredients of grace. For they are the ways in which we are very likely to sense the God at work in our lives.

Or it may be that we need to distinguish between active and passive modes of grace. One of the infirmities of grace defined as acceptance is that it too often suggests a kind of benevolent tolerance on the part of God rather than divine zeal for the salvation of every human soul. The God of the Bible does not sit back on some remote throne and cluck a patient tongue at the follies of the race, but follows sinners to the ends of the earth, "the uttermost parts of the sea" and into the very depths of Sheol itself. Whatever the word *acceptance* may mean to sophisticated theologians, it does not begin to measure such love in the minds of lay men and women. The equation of grace with the divine determination to let none escape into self-destruction lends dignity to human life and to the relationship of creature with Creator.

But whether it is some such distinction as these or another way of discussing the subject, preachers need to show far more determination than most have had in the past in relating faith and works in the experience of the laity.

The second element in the content of new being that needs more thoughtful proclamation is the recognition of just how truly social the gospel must be. And it follows quite naturally from what I have just been saying about faith and works.

Just as it is folly to suppose that one can talk about Christian commitment without talking about concrete actions and specific relationships, so it is not only absurd but cruel to imply that faithful behavior is independent of social structure and process.

It has always seemed to me that one of the infirmities of most of the social action preaching that I have heard has been its tendency to define that action as a duty which the believer is obligated to take seriously because of what needs to be done for the poor and the deprived of this world. That is, people are urged as an expression of their faith to make society more humane for others.

Now that is, of course, a valid and tremendously important aspect of the whole problem. I have no wish to denigrate or underestimate it at all. But in its homiletic, as distinct from its academic expression, too little has been said about the importance of social action as the medium by which all believers, including the rich and the powerful, can be enabled to lead more deeply fulfilling lives. The great prophetic preachers of the first half of this century said much that needed to be said about what the faithful are summoned to do for others and about the amendments in social processes by which these reforms might be made possible.

When one leaves the books on the subject, however, and inspects the sermons which they inspired, one finds very little about the kinds of institutional changes which might be required if the "haves" as well as the "have-nots" are to discern the content of new being. And while the problem of the "haves" differs from that of the "have-nots" in many ways, it can be even more spiritually debilitating, more corrosive to the human soul.

How, for example, might one relate the gospel to a young man or woman who must on Monday morning go back to work in a factory in which homicidal experiments in germ warfare are being carried out? Or, to put the question somewhat less dramatically but more relevantly for most of us, how does one proclaim the gospel faithfully to people whose daily work requires them to develop more persuasive ways of deceiving the public into buying useless, shoddy, or downright dangerous products? Such men and women are perishing in their own way every bit as surely as are those afflicted by hunger, disease, and political oppression. To speak to them as though they enjoy a moral autonomy, a range of options within their jobs, does them less than no good and makes our preaching seem absurd.

It is easy enough to sit at one's desk in a theological seminary and work out all kinds of rationalizations in this matter. I know, because I have done it often. But it is quite another thing to stand in the pulpit week after week and preach to the used car dealer, his wife who writes advertising copy for a large tobacco firm, or the inconspicuous person in the back pew who spends eight hours every day pressing a pedal on the machine that turns out schlock. They know what is happening to them. And when we seem not to know our preaching is in vain.

It is not enough to acknowledge that the Christian faith has social implications. What is needed in the pulpit today is the insistence that it has inescapable and inherent social dimensions. And that will call for a kind of theologizing that can be done only by those who are actually at work in the church's front line.

One December afternoon many years ago a group of parents stood in the lobby of a nursery school waiting to pick up their children after the last pre-Christmas session. As the youngsters ran from their lockers, each one carried in his or her hands the "surprise," the brightly wrapped package on which the class had been working for weeks.

One small boy, trying to run, put on his coat, and wave to his parents all at the same time, slipped and fell. The "surprise" flew from his grasp and landed on the tile floor with an obvious ceramic crash.

The child's first reaction was one of stunned silence. But then he set up an inconsolable wail. His father, thinking to minimize the incident and comfort the boy, patted his head and murmured, "Now that's all right. It really doesn't matter, son. It doesn't matter at all."

But the child's mother, somewhat wiser in such situations, dropped to her knees on the floor, swept the boy into her arms and said, "Oh, but it does matter. It matters a great deal." And she wept with her son.

The redeeming God in whom we hope is not the parent who dismisses our lives with a pat on the head and murmured assurances that they do not really matter in cosmic terms. It is, rather, the one who falls to the earth beside us, picks up our torn and bleeding spirits, and says, "Oh, but it does matter. It matters eternally."

# Some Theses
## for
### Preachers

1. Effective Christian preaching distinguishes carefully among the following:
   a. the *individual experience of God* in daily life;
   b. *religion* as the internal and social structuring of that experience;
   c. *theology* as the professional vocabulary of scholars in the field of religion.
2. Neither religion nor theology fully expresses the human experience of God. Each can only help men and women relate their experience to the experiences of other people and other times.
3. Most lay men and women have little sustained interest in theology and only a superficial interest in religion. They care deeply about the experience of God, whatever they may chose to call it.
4. The human experience of God is as complex as the life in which it occurs. It cannot be made simple without the loss of depth.
5. The complexity of life in history is the primary result of the Fall and reflects humanity's separation from that fullness of truth that is the immediate presence of God.
6. Preaching which offers simple answers to life's complex dilemmas undermines the essential quality of truly human being, that is, the fragmentary vision of truth.
7. The fragmentary vision of truth is the basis of human freedom, because it prevents the individual will from being overpowered by a full knowledge of the divine.
8. The human demand for simplicity in preaching is one of the

most dangerous forms of sinfulness, since it seeks to cut God down to manageable proportions.

9. The complexity of the life in faith can be dealt with in preaching, provided that:
   a. the subject is divided into bite-sized chunks;
   b. each sermon is carefully prepared.

10. Preaching effectively within the complex human experience of God the Creator, Judge, and Redeemer begins with the recognition that manifestations of the Eternal will always seem somewhat at odds with one another when viewed in finite perspective.

11. The most fundamental thing the Bible tells us about God is that the Creator has fashioned human beings as the instrumentalities of divine creativity within history.

12. It is a primary responsibility of preaching to help men and women understand the origin and nature of their own creative energies. Much of what must be known about the divine will springs from that understanding.

13. The Bible tells us that God is our Judge as well as our Creator and that in the tension between form and energy one discerns the Old Testament's definition of history.

14. The endless tension that is history causes much human suffering which is inexplicable so long as the origin and nature of that tension are ignored.

15. The creating and judging God is revealed in the particular data of human experience, which take on significance and are consecrated by the divine presence. Thus, a piety which seeks to transcend the particular and relate to God in autonomous moments threatens the pious with dehumanization.

16. The affirmation of divine judgment is the sine qua non to the proclamation of God's mercy. Mercy that is preached outside the context of judgment is grace trivialized.

17. When rightly understood, judgment gives structure and dignity to human existence. Lay men and women understand this and can be demoralized rather than comforted by preaching which overemphasizes unequivocal compassion.

18. The current proclamation of divine "acceptance" contributes significantly to the anomie characteristic of our time, because it suggests the lack of consequence in relative human achievements.

19. Preaching a biblical concept of judgment will do more to counter irrational fears of hell than endless assurances of divine compassion.

20. God's mercy is manifest in the healing love which makes rebirth possible at every juncture in life.

21. The divine compassion incarnate in Jesus Christ inevitably seems irresponsible within history, because it defies historical structures of order and negates the causalities of human justice. Therefore, sermonic exhortations to "emulate the Master in all things" are counsels of futility.

22. God's promise of life eternal is the assurance that what is seen fragmentarily, "in a glass darkly," in history will be revealed as a harmonious whole beyond the limitations of time and space.